GOD'S ANSWERS
for LIFE'S
NEEDS

Other Books by Paul E. Engle

Baker's Funeral Handbook

Baker's Wedding Handbook

Baker's Worship Handbook

Discovering the Fullness of Worship

The Governor Drove Us Up the Wall

Guarding and Growing

Worship Planbook

GOD'S ANSWERS
for LIFE'S NEEDS

PAUL E. ENGLE AND MARGIE W. ENGLE

Baker Books

A Division of Baker Book House Co
Grand Rapids, Michigan 49516

Published by Baker Books
a division of Baker Book House Company
P.O. Box 6287, Grand Rapids, MI 49516-6287

Printed in the United States of America

Library of Congress Cataloging-in-Publication Data

Engle, Paul E.
    God's answers for life's needs / Paul E. Engle and Margie W. Engle.
        p. cm.
    ISBN 0-8010-6326-4
    1. Bible—Quotations. I. Engle, Margie W., 1946– II. Title.
BS432.E54 2000
220.6—dc21   00-027892

Unless otherwise marked, Scripture quotations are from the King James Version of the Bible.

Scripture quotations marked NASB are from the NEW AMERICAN STANDARD BIBLE ®. Copyright © The Lockman Foundation 1960, 1962, 1963, 1968, 1971, 1972, 1973, 1975, 1977, 1995. Used by permission.

Scripture quotations marked NIV are from the HOLY BIBLE, NEW INTERNATIONAL VERSION®. NIV®. Copyright © 1973, 1978, 1984 by International Bible Society. Used by permission of Zondervan Publishing House. All rights reserved.

Scripture quotations marked NKJV are from the New King James Version. Copyright © 1979, 1980, 1982 by Thomas Nelson, Inc. Used by permission. All rights reserved.

Scripture quotations marked NLT are from the *Holy Bible,* New Living Translation, copyright © 1996. Used by permission of Tyndale House Publishers, Inc., Wheaton, IL 60189. All rights reserved.

For current information about all releases from Baker Book House, visit our web site:
http://www.bakerbooks.com

Christine and Dana

Heather and Phil

May Scripture continue
to be your compass
throughout life's journey.

CONTENTS

HOW TO USE THIS BOOK

We live in a postbiblical era in which general knowledge of the Bible can no longer be assumed—both within and without the church. Not surprisingly, this decline in biblical knowledge is accompanied by a corresponding inability to use the Bible in practical ways to find answers to life's daily needs. Many people today turn to pop culture icons, newspaper horoscopes, motivational seminars, or on-line chat rooms instead of the Bible.

The Bible was never intended to be a closed book within leather covers, opened only by the clergy on Sundays within the walls of a church. Scripture is God's gift to equip each of us to face the entire range of situations that arise throughout life's journey (see 2 Tim. 3:16). Financial pressures, illness, interpersonal conflicts, natural disaster, rebellious children, temptations, and the myriad other situations that fill our days should drive us to the Scripture in which we find our center of gravity.

God's people throughout history have looked to Scripture as a source of comfort, encouragement, and reliable wisdom because it is God's inspired and living Word. J. B. Phillips tells in his book *Ring of Truth* how he discovered, when translating the Greek text of the New Testament into contemporary English, that "although I did my utmost to preserve an emotional detachment, I find again and again that the material under my hands was strangely alive; it

spoke to my condition in the most uncanny way" (p. 25).
Scripture still speaks to us in the twenty-first century.

Why Was This Book Written?

God's Answers for Life's Needs was written to provide a
practical tool to quickly summarize what the Bible teaches
about thirty-two common situations from daily life. Each
chapter provides the following:

- A series of summary statements outlining the Bible's
  teaching on various life needs or situations.

- Selected significant Scripture verses from five different translations relating to each summary statement.

- A personal prayer to guide one's thoughts in praying
  for each need or situation.

- A biblical promise to claim and on which to meditate.

- A quotation from a Christian leader relating to each
  subject.

We need to clarify that this book intentionally includes
only selected verses rather than exhaustive information on
each topic. We trust that its readers will be motivated to
open their Bibles and read entire passages in context. God
often chooses, however, to use selected small portions of
Scripture to minister to our spirits in the midst of life's trials. As Margaret Clarkson observes in her book *Grace
Grows Best in Winter:*

> Here fragments of the Word frequently serve a special purpose
> in the Spirit's ministry. As myriad drops of dew reflect the sun's
> rays, each with a similar yet totally differing glory, so tiny bits and

pieces of Scripture reflect new faces of radiance from long-loved truths to illumine new phases of old sorrows and meet our recurring needs. It is both easy and perilous to neglect or ignore such fragmentary sources of nourishment when we may not have the food to which we are accustomed; we must not despise the day of small things. Fragments of Scripture in the hand of God can minister to our spirits and sustain us through many trials: let us learn to seek them out and use them.

pages 27–28

What Are Some Ways This Book Can Be Used?

- If you are facing one or more of the thirty-two life situations mentioned in this book, we trust that reading, rereading, and reflecting on the biblical insight given will prove to be a source of encouragement and direction that enables you to face your problems biblically.

- If you are looking for new material to use for devotional reading, you may find this book refreshing and helpful.

- If you have a friend, neighbor, or relative struggling through some difficult times, you may wish to consider lending or purchasing for them a copy of this book as a practical way of showing concern for them.

- If you are requested to give counsel or advice to someone who is going through one or more of the situations covered in this book, you might find it helpful to refer to the content of this book in conversations with them.

- If you are called upon to give a devotional message in a group setting, you might find that the topical

11

outlines in each chapter provide the structure for thoughts to share in speaking to the group.

- If you have friends who have not yet made a personal commitment to Christ, you may wish to provide them with a copy of the book and encourage them to look at the opening chapter.

- If someone you know has recently made a commitment to Christ and desires to learn how to use Scripture in practical ways in daily life, this guide to Scripture would be a valuable tool to use in discipling a new convert.

A. W. Tozer once remarked, "I have always felt that when we read and study the Word of God, we should have great expectations. We should ask the Holy Spirit to reveal the person, the glory and the eternal ministry of our Lord Jesus Christ." It is our prayer that you will meditate on the Scripture references in this book with a keen expectation that God will use his timeless, inspired Word to directly address your deepest needs. May you experience God's sustaining grace in a fresh way, and may the fragments of Scripture minister to your spirit and sustain you through all the circumstances of your life's journey.

BECOMING A CHRISTIAN

*Only Christianity provides true redemption—a restoration
to our created state and the hope of eternal peace with
God. No other worldview identifies the real problem: the
stain of sin in our souls. No other worldview can set free a
tormented soul. . . . And having been liberated from sin, we
are empowered to help bring Christ's restoration to the entire creation order.*

—Charles Colson and Nancy Pearcey, *How Now Should We Live?*

1. A caring God created us to know him and live in relationship with him.

➳ He has planted eternity in the human heart.

Ecclesiastes 3:11 NLT

➳ Then God said, "Let Us make man in Our image, according
to Our likeness; let them have dominion over the fish of the sea,
over the birds of the air, and over the cattle, over all the earth
and over every creeping thing that creeps on the earth." So God

created man in His own image; in the image of God He created
him; male and female He created them.

Genesis 1:26–27 KJV

⤙ God, for whom and through whom everything exists.

Hebrews 2:10b NIV

⤙ He is the God who made the world and everything in it. Since
he is Lord of heaven and earth, he doesn't live in man-made tem-
ples, and human hands can't serve his needs—for he has no
needs. He himself gives life and breath to everything, and he satisfies every need there is. . . . His purpose in all of this was that
the nations should seek after God and perhaps feel their way toward him and find him—though he is not far from any one of
us. For in him we live and move and exist.

Acts 17:24–25, 27–28 NLT

⤙ That which is known about God is evident within them; for
God made it evident to them. For since the creation of the world
His invisible attributes, His eternal power and divine nature, have
been clearly seen, being understood through what has been
made, so that they are without excuse.

Romans 1:19–20 NASB

**2. Selfish ambition drives many to accept the common lie
that God can be ignored in this life with no consequences
in the next. The root of this human condition is sin.**

⤙ The fool has said in his heart, "There is no God."

Psalm 14:1 NASB

⤙ No one is good—not even one. No one has real understanding; no one is seeking God. All have turned away from God; all
have gone wrong. No one does good, not even one. . . . They have
no fear of God to restrain them. . . . For all have sinned; all fall
short of God's glorious standard.

Romans 3:10–12, 18, 23 NLT

14

⇥ For even though they knew God, they did not honor Him as God or give thanks, but they became futile in their speculations, and their foolish heart was darkened.

Romans 1:21 NASB

3. This condition of sin has serious consequences, including interpersonal conflict, lack of meaning and direction in life, and the prospect of eternal punishment and separation from God.

⇥ "Whoever rejects the Son will not see life, for God's wrath remains on him."

John 3:36b NIV

⇥ Now the deeds of the flesh are evident, which are: immorality, impurity, sensuality, idolatry, sorcery, enmities, strife, jealousy, outbursts of anger, disputes, dissensions, factions, envying, drunkenness, carousing, and things like these, of which I forewarn you, just as I have forewarned you, that those who practice such things will not inherit the kingdom of God.

Galatians 5:19–21 NASB

⇥ For the wages of sin is death.

Romans 6:23a NKJV

4. God's solution to this universal human dilemma was to send his Son to earth to live a perfect life, to die an undeserved death assuming the punishment we deserve, and to experience a physical resurrection, in order that our relationship with our creator could be eternally restored. Christ's initiative was absolutely necessary because no human efforts to restore this relationship could be sufficient.

⇥ "For God so loved the world that He gave His only begotten Son, that whoever believes in Him should not perish but have everlasting life. For God did not send His Son into the world

15

to condemn the world, but that the world through Him might be saved."

John 3:16–17 NKJV

✴ But God demonstrates His own love toward us, in that while we were still sinners, Christ died for us.

Romans 5:8 NKJV

✴ I passed on to you what was most important and what had also been passed on to me—that Christ died for our sins, just as the Scriptures said. He was buried, and he was raised from the dead on the third day, as the Scriptures said.

1 Corinthians 15:3–4 NLT

✴ For it is by grace you have been saved, through faith—and this not from yourselves, it is the gift of God—not by works, so that no one can boast.

Ephesians 2:8–9 NIV

✴ But when the kindness and love of God our Savior appeared, he saved us, not because of righteous things we had done, but because of his mercy.

Titus 3:4–5 NIV

5. God's offer of new life through Christ calls for our response. As we turn from our sinful past and place our trust in Christ alone for forgiveness, we are freely pardoned and joyfully welcomed into God's family.

✴ Let the wicked forsake his way and the evil man his thoughts. Let him turn to the LORD, and he will have mercy on him, and to our God, for he will freely pardon.

Isaiah 55:7 NIV

✴ "Believe in the Lord Jesus, and you will be saved."

Acts 16:31 NASB

✴ But to all who believed him and accepted him, he gave the right to become children of God. They are reborn! This is not a physical birth resulting from human passion or plan—this rebirth comes from God.

John 1:12–13 NLT

If you confess with your mouth, "Jesus is Lord," and believe in your heart that God raised him from the dead, you will be saved. For it is with your heart that you believe and are justified, and it is with your mouth that you confess and are saved.

Romans 10:9–10 NIV

Prayer

Father, I long to enter into a life made new and alive by your Spirit. I confess that I have willfully and deliberately sinned against you and am in need of your cleansing. I believe that your Son died on the cross and shed his blood to pay the penalty for my sin and to bridge the gap between you and me. I hereby place my trust in Christ as my Savior and receive the forgiveness that you have made possible. I joyfully surrender my life to your control and ask that you would guide me as I take my first baby steps of faith.

Promise

"Believe in the Lord Jesus, and you will be saved."

Acts 16:31 NASB

BIRTH IN THE FAMILY

Thank you for children
brought into being
because we loved.
God of love
keep us loving
so that they
may grow up whole
in love's overflow.

—Joseph Bayly,
Psalms of My Life

1. The Lord oversees and facilitates the complex workmanship of forming each child in the womb.

᷍ You made all the delicate, inner parts of my body and knit me together in my mother's womb. Thank you for making me so wonderfully complex! Your workmanship is marvelous—and how well I know it. You watched me as I was being formed in utter seclusion, as I was woven together in the dark of the womb. You saw me before I was born. Every day of my life was recorded in your book. Every moment was laid out before a single day had passed.

Psalm 139:13–16 NLT

2. The Lord determines the appropriate timing for the birth of each child.

↜ Before I formed you in the womb I knew you; before you were born I sanctified you.

Jeremiah 1:5 NKJV

↜ To every thing there is a season, and a time to every purpose under the heaven: A time to be born, and a time to die.

Ecclesiastes 3:1–2

↜ Sarah conceived and bore a son to Abraham in his old age, at the appointed time of which God had spoken to him.

Genesis 21:2 NASB

3. The birth of a child is often in answer to the earnest prayers of parents.

↜ Isaac prayed to the LORD on behalf of his wife, because she was barren; and the LORD answered him and Rebekah his wife conceived.

Genesis 25:21 NASB

↜ She, greatly distressed, prayed to the LORD and wept bitterly. . . . It came about in due time, after Hannah had conceived, that she gave birth to a son; and she named him Samuel, saying, "Because I have asked him of the LORD. . . . For this boy I prayed, and the LORD has given me my petition which I asked of Him. So I have also dedicated him to the LORD; as long as he lives he is dedicated to the LORD."

1 Samuel 1:10, 20, 27–28 NASB

19

↵ But the angel said to him: "Do not be afraid, Zechariah; your prayer has been heard. Your wife Elizabeth will bear you a son, and you are to give him the name John."

Luke 1:13 NIV

4. Each child should be viewed as a gift and reward from the Lord.

↵ Children born to a young man are like sharp arrows in a warrior's hands. How happy is the man whose quiver is full of them! He will not be put to shame when he confronts his accusers at the city gates.

Psalm 127:4–5 NLT

5. The birth of a child can be an occasion of joyful celebration for family and friends.

↵ "You will have joy and gladness, and many will rejoice at his birth." . . . When her neighbors and relatives heard how the Lord had shown great mercy to her, they rejoiced with her.

Luke 1:14, 58 NKJV

6. During his earthly ministry Christ revealed a high view of children.

↵ And they were bringing children to Him so that He might touch them; but the disciples rebuked them. But when Jesus saw this, He was indignant and said to them, "Permit the children to come to Me; do not hinder them; for the kingdom of God belongs to such as these. Truly I say to you, whoever does not receive the kingdom of God like a child will not enter it at all." And he took them in His arms and began blessing them, laying His hands on them.

Mark 10:13–16 NASB

↵ "And whoever welcomes a little child like this in my name welcomes me. But if anyone causes one of these little ones who believe in me to sin, it would be better for him to have a large

20

millstone hung around his neck and to be drowned in the depths of the sea."

Matthew 18:5–6 NIV

7. God ordained worship and praise to come from the lips of infants and children.

From the lips of children and infants you have ordained praise because of your enemies, to silence the foe and the avenger.

Psalm 8:2 NIV (see also Matt. 21:16)

Prayer

Father, You are the giver of every good and perfect gift, and my heart is exploding with joy today because of the treasure I hold in my arms. Surely no language on earth contains enough words to express the feelings of gratitude that well up inside me. I am in awe of the miracle I cradle in my arms. To think that the life that I hold is made in your image is beyond what I can fully fathom. If only this child will grow to recognize your image in me, I could have no greater joy. Thank you for entrusting me with this precious life to nurture in reverence. Thank you that the birth of this child enables me to understand in the smallest of ways at what great cost you sacrificed the Son that you loved. I pray this prayer in the name of the one who sees in my child the very kingdom of heaven.

Promise

"Permit the children to come to Me; do not hinder them; for the kingdom of God belongs to such as these."

Mark 10:14 NASB

BURNOUT AND EXHAUSTION

A. B. Simpson, approaching middle age, broken in health, deeply despondent and ready to quit the ministry, chanced to hear the simple spiritual, "Nothing is too hard for Jesus, No man can work like Him." Its message sped like an arrow to his heart, carrying faith and hope and life for body and soul. He sought a place of retirement and after a season alone with God arose to his feet completely cured, and went forth in fullness of joy to found what has since become one of the largest foreign missionary societies in the world. For thirty-five years after this encounter with God he labored prodigiously in the service of Christ. His faith in the God of limitless power gave him all the strength he needed to carry on.

—A. W. Tozer, *The Knowledge of the Holy*

1. The prophet Elijah experienced severe burnout and exhaustion after his confrontation with the prophets of Baal. He pleaded with God that his life be taken.

➤ He himself went a day's journey into the wilderness, and came and sat down under a broom tree. And he prayed that he might die, and said, "It is enough! Now, LORD, take my life, for I am no better than my fathers. . . . I have been very zealous for the LORD God of hosts; for the children of Israel have forsaken Your covenant, torn down Your altars, and killed Your prophets with the sword. I alone am left; and they seek to take my life."

1 Kings 19:4, 10 NKJV

2. The Lord reached out to Elijah in his state of weakness and discouragement and restored him to productive ministry.

➤ So he arose, and ate and drank; and he went in the strength of that food forty days and forty nights as far as Horeb, the mountain of God. . . . Go out and stand on the mountain before the LORD. And behold, the LORD passed by, and a great and strong wind tore into the mountains and broke the rocks in pieces before the LORD, but the LORD was not in the wind; and after the wind an earthquake, but the LORD was not in the earthquake; and after the earthquake a fire, but the LORD was not in the fire; and after the fire a still small voice.

1 Kings 19:8, 11–12 NKJV

3. Samson's disobedience and sinful relationships resulted in the loss of his unusual strength.

➤ So he told her all that was in his heart and said to her, "A razor has never come on my head, for I have been a Nazirite to God from my mother's womb. If I am shaved, then my strength will leave me and I will become weak and be like any other man." . . . She said, The Philistines are upon you, Samson! And he awoke from his sleep and said, "I will go out as at other times and shake myself free." But he did not know that the LORD had departed from him. Then the Philistines seized him and gouged out his eyes;

23

and they brought him down to Gaza and bound him with bronze chains, and he was a grinder in the prison.

Judges 16:17, 20–21 NASB

4. Samson's strength was restored by the Lord in answer to his earnest prayer.

Then Samson called to the LORD and said, "O Lord GOD, please remember me and please strengthen me just this time, O God, that I may at once be avenged of the Philistines for my two eyes." Samson grasped the two middle pillars on which the house rested, and braced himself against them, the one with his right hand and the other with his left. And Samson said, "Let me die with the Philistines!" And he bent with all his might so that the house fell on the lords and all the people who were in it. So the dead whom he killed at his death were more than those whom he killed in his life.

Judges 16:28–30 NASB

5. David's unconfessed sin left him drained of strength.

I am dying from grief; my years are shortened by sadness. Misery [or sin] has drained my strength; I am wasting away from within.

Psalm 31:10 NLT

When I kept silent, my bones wasted away through my groaning all day long. For day and night your hand was heavy upon me; my strength was sapped as in the heat of summer.

Psalm 32:3–4 NIV

A raging fever burns within me, and my health is broken. I am exhausted and completely crushed. My groans come from an anguished heart. . . . My heart beats wildly, my strength fails, and I am going blind.

Psalm 38:7–8, 10 NLT

6. God's strength is available to his people in old age.

↝ Do not cast me off in the time of old age; Do not forsake me when my strength fails. . . . I will go in the strength of the Lord GOD. . . . Now also when I am old and grayheaded, O God, do not forsake me, until I declare Your strength to this generation, Your power to everyone who is to come.

Psalm 71:9, 16, 18 NKJV

7. Scripture repeatedly encourages us to look to the Lord as the source of the strength we need to overcome weakness.

↝ The joy of the LORD is your strength.

Nehemiah 8:10

↝ I will love thee, O LORD, my strength.

Psalm 18:1

↝ The LORD is the strength of my life; of whom shall I be afraid?

Psalm 27:1

↝ The LORD is my strength and my shield; my heart trusted in him, and I am helped: therefore my heart greatly rejoiceth; and with my song will I praise him.

Psalm 28:7

↝ When I pray, you answer me; you encourage me by giving me the strength I need.

Psalm 138:3 NLT

↝ I can do all things through Christ which strengtheneth me.

Philippians 4:13

8. The Lord can use our weakness to display his strength.

⟊ But God chose the foolish things of the world to shame the wise; God chose the weak things of the world to shame the strong.

1 Corinthians 1:27 NIV

⟊ I take pleasure in infirmities, in reproaches, in necessities, in persecutions, in distresses for Christ's sake: for when I am weak, then am I strong.

2 Corinthians 12:10

9. The Lord's supply of strength is never exhausted and is available to his people who wait with confidence.

⟊ Have you never heard or understood? Don't you know that the LORD is the everlasting God, the Creator of all the earth? He never grows faint or weary. No one can measure the depths of his understanding. He gives power to those who are tired and worn out; he offers strength to the weak. Even youths will become exhausted, and young men will give up. But those who wait on the LORD will find new strength. They will fly high on wings like eagles. They will run and not grow weary. They will walk and not faint.

Isaiah 40:28–31 NLT

10. God expects us to reach out to our brothers and sisters in their times of weakness.

⟊ In everything I showed you that by working hard in this manner you must help the weak and remember the words of the Lord Jesus, that He Himself said, "It is more blessed to give than to receive."

Acts 20:35 NASB

⟊ Now we exhort you, brethren, warn those who are unruly, comfort the fainthearted, uphold the weak, be patient with all.

1 Thessalonians 5:14 NKJV

Prayer

Lord, I am ready to throw in the towel. The energy and enthusiasm I once had for life are a thing of the past. The physical and emotional resources I once relied upon are completely spent.

Once again, my inadequacy has brought me back to home port. I cast myself upon your loving mercy and pray that you would deliver me from this overwhelming feeling of uselessness and helplessness. Correct my focus and renew my relationship to you. Restore to me the joy of my salvation, and enable me to dedicate the remaining days and years of my life to proclaiming your love.

Promise

Have you never heard or understood? Don't you know that the LORD is the everlasting God, the Creator of all the earth? He never grows faint or weary. No one can measure the depths of his understanding. He gives power to those who are tired and worn out; he offers strength to the weak.

Isaiah 40:28–29 NLT

DISCIPLINING AND TRAINING OUR CHILDREN

It's a manifest fact that we are creatures of extremes. Invariably we suffer from the peril of the pendulum. Too many parents assume the role of a Simon Legree. They nail the kid to the floor every time he squeaks; they make a federal case out of every misdemeanor. Others become overly permissive, paralyzed by their child's behavior, scared to death to lay a hand on him for fear of permanently damaging his psyche.

—Howard G. Hendricks, *Heaven Help the Home*

1. God has entrusted parents with the responsibility to pass on their faith to the next generation.

➤ "You must commit yourselves wholeheartedly to these commands I am giving you today. Repeat them again and again to your children. Talk about them when you are at home and when you are away on a journey, when you are lying down and when you are getting up again. Tie them to your hands as a reminder, and wear them on your forehead. Write them on the doorposts of your house and on your gates."

Deuteronomy 6:6–9 NLT

⤝ Fathers, do not provoke your children to anger, but bring them up in the discipline and instruction of the Lord.

Ephesians 6:4 NASB

⤝ For I am mindful of the sincere faith within you, which first dwelt in your grandmother Lois and your mother Eunice, and I am sure that it is in you as well. . . . from childhood you have known the sacred writings which are able to give you the wisdom that leads to salvation through faith which is in Christ Jesus.

2 Timothy 1:5, 3:15 NASB

2. God has also entrusted parents with the loving discipline of their children.

⤝ Fathers, do not exasperate your children; instead, bring them up in the training and instruction of the Lord.

Ephesians 6:4 NIV

⤝ Fathers, do not embitter your children, or they will become discouraged.

Colossians 3:21 NIV

⤝ He who spares his rod hates his son, but he who loves him disciplines him promptly.

Proverbs 13:24 NKJV

⤝ Do not withhold correction from a child, for if you beat him with a rod, he will not die. You shall beat him with a rod, and deliver his soul from hell.

Proverbs 23:13–14 NKJV

3. Just as God's discipline of us his children is motivated by love, so should the discipline of our children be carried out with love.

↗ Know then in your heart that as a man disciplines his son, so the LORD your God disciplines you.

Deuteronomy 8:5 NIV

↗ For the LORD corrects those he loves, just as a father corrects a child in whom he delights.

Proverbs 3:12 NLT

↗ As many as I love, I rebuke and chasten.

Revelation 3:19

↗ And have you entirely forgotten the encouraging words God spoke to you, his children? He said, "My child, don't ignore it when the Lord disciplines you, and don't be discouraged when he corrects you. For the Lord disciplines those he loves, and he punishes those he accepts as his children." . . . Whoever heard of a child who was never disciplined? . . . Since we respect our earthly fathers who disciplined us, should we not all the more cheerfully submit to the discipline of our heavenly Father and live forever? For our earthly fathers disciplined us for a few years, doing the best they know how. But God's discipline is always right and good for us because it means we will share in his holiness.

Hebrews 12:5–7, 9–10 NLT

4. God expects that Christian leaders will manage their children and households well.

↗ He must be one who manages his own household well, keeping his children under control with all dignity. . . . Deacons must be husbands of only one wife, and good managers of their children and their own households.

1 Timothy 3:4, 12 NASB

↗ Having faithful children not accused of dissipation or insubordination.

Titus 1:6 NKJV

5. Parents who faithfully discipline their children often reap a rich blessing.

‿ Discipline your son, and he will give you peace; he will bring delight to your soul.

Proverbs 29:17 NIV

‿ Discipline your children while there is hope. If you don't, you will ruin their lives.

Proverbs 19:18 NLT

‿ Her children arise and call her blessed; her husband also, and he praises her.

Proverbs 31:28 NIV

6. Failure to obey parents is foolish and can lead to heartache.

‿ A fool despises his father's instruction, but he who receives reproof is prudent. . . . A wise son makes his father glad, but a foolish man despises his mother.

Proverbs 15:5, 20 NKJV

‿ He who curses his father or his mother, his lamp will go out in time of darkness.

Proverbs 20:20 NASB

‿ The eye that mocks a father and scorns a mother, the ravens of the valley will pick it out, and the young eagles will eat it.

Proverbs 30:17 NASB

‿ You should also know this, Timothy, that in the last days there will be very difficult times. For people will be . . . disobedient to their parents.

2 Timothy 3:1–2 NLT

7. God requires that children obey their parents in the Lord.

31

᠊᠊ Listen to your father who begot you, and do not despise your mother when she is old.

Proverbs 23:22 NKJV

᠊᠊ Children, obey your parents in the Lord, for this is right. "Honor your father and mother"—which is the first commandment with a promise—"that it may go well with you and that you may enjoy long life on the earth."

Ephesians 6:1–3 NIV

᠊᠊ You children must always obey your parents, for this is what pleases the Lord.

Colossians 3:20 NLT

Prayer

Lord, I do not always appreciate your chastening rod in my life. Neither do my children always respond with appreciation to my human attempts to provide instruction and correction in their lives. O God, it would be so much easier if children could raise themselves! But that was never your plan.

Remind me when the going is rough that parenting is not a popularity contest. By your grace, enable me to discipline in love, to listen, to encourage, to instruct, and to share God intimately with my family. I want my children to know they are not an intrusion in my life but are cherished gifts from God. When discipline is required, help me to show my children the same spirit of love and forgiveness you have shown me.

Promise

Discipline your son, and he will give you peace; he will bring delight to your soul.

Proverbs 29:17 NIV

DISCOVERING OUR GIFTS

Like seeds or babies, spiritual gifts start small and grow with proper care. Constant usage coupled with love and dependence on the Holy Spirit gradually develop them into effective instruments. In developing his gifts, the servant of God becomes useful himself. His gifts fit his personality, temperament and background and to some extent shape his future, for the gifts give guidance as to the type of service the Holy Spirit wants each Christian to perform.

—Charles Mylander, *How to Discover Your Spiritual Gifts*

1. **Every Christian is the recipient of one or more spiritual gifts.**

➤ But the manifestation of the Spirit is given to each one for the profit of all.

1 Corinthians 12:7 NKJV

➤ Distributing to each one individually as He wills.

1 Corinthians 12:11 NKJV

33

2. The Holy Spirit sovereignly distributes these gifts as he pleases, not on the basis of any human merit.

All these are the work of one and the same Spirit, and he gives them to each one, just as he determines.

1 Corinthians 12:11 NIV

Since we have gifts that differ according to the grace given to us, each of us is to exercise them accordingly.

Romans 12:6 NASB

3. A rich variety of spiritual gifts is mentioned in Scripture in representative rather than exhaustive listings.

Gifts listed in Scripture: message of wisdom, utterance of knowledge, faith, healing, miraculous powers, prophecy, discrimination between spirits, tongues, ability to interpret tongues, serving, teaching, encouragement, generosity, leadership, mercy, speaking.

1 Corinthians 12:4–6, 8–10; Romans 12:6–8; 1 Peter 4:11

4. The purpose of spiritual gifts is not for selfish gratification but for service to others.

The manifestation of the Spirit is given to each one for the profit of all.

1 Corinthians 12:7 NKJV

Each one should use whatever gift he has received to serve others, faithfully administering God's grace in its various forms.

1 Peter 4:10 NIV

Under his direction, the whole body is fitted together perfectly. As each part does its own special work, it helps the other parts grow, so that the whole body is healthy and growing and full of love.

Ephesians 4:16 NLT

5. The result of exercising our spiritual gifts should be that God is glorified through Jesus Christ.

☙ Whoever speaks, let him speak, as it were, the utterances of God; whoever serves, let him do so as by the strength which God supplies; so that in all things God may be glorified through Jesus Christ, to whom belongs the glory and dominion forever and ever. Amen.

1 Peter 4:11 NASB

6. Spiritual gifts are misused if they are not exercised with love.

☙ If I could speak in any language in heaven or on earth but didn't love others, I would only be making meaningless noise like a loud gong or a clanging cymbal.

1 Corinthians 13:1 NLT

☙ Let love be your highest goal, but also desire the special abilities the Spirit gives, especially the gift of prophecy.

1 Corinthians 14:1 NLT

7. It is essential that we actively exercise our spiritual gifts rather than neglect them.

☙ Do not neglect the spiritual gift within you.

1 Timothy 4:14 NASB

☙ I remind you to kindle afresh the gift of God which is in you through the laying on of my hands.

2 Timothy 1:6 NASB

Prayer

Father, thank you that in your sovereignty you have distributed an orchestra of gifts to your children to be used for ministry to

the body of Christ and to advance its witness in the world. Forgive me for times when I have been tempted to shelve my gifts
or casually lay them aside. By your grace enable me to develop
and deploy each of the gifts you have given me in concert with
the gifts you have given others within the church. May your
church be mobilized and its members drawn together in fellowship and love as the gifts of your people are exercised in mutual
interdependence. I offer this prayer in the name of the giver of
all good and perfect gifts.

Promise

All these are the work of one and the same Spirit, and he gives them
to each one, just as he determines.

1 Corinthians 12:11 NIV

EXPERIENCING GOD'S LOVE

Is it true that God is love to me as a Christian? And does the love of God mean all that has been said? If so, certain questions arise. Why do I ever grumble and show discontent and resentment at the circumstances in which God has placed me? Why am I ever distrustful, fearful, or depressed? Why do I ever allow myself to grow cool, formal, and half-hearted in the service of the God who loves me so? Why do I ever allow my loyalties to be divided, so that God has not all my heart?

—J. I. Packer, *Knowing God*

1. The Lord God expects that we love him with all our being.

⁓ Love the LORD your God with all your heart and with all your soul and with all your strength.

Deuteronomy 6:5 NIV

⁓ "You shall love the LORD your God with all your heart, with all your soul, and with all your mind. This is the first and great commandment. And the second is like it: You shall love your neighbor as yourself. On these two commandments hang all the Law and the Prophets."

Matthew 22:37–40 NKJV

﹏ And now, Israel, what does the LORD your God require of you, but to fear the LORD your God, to walk in all His ways and to love Him, to serve the LORD your God with all your heart and with all your soul, and to keep the commandments of the LORD and His statutes which I command you today for your good?

Deuteronomy 10:12–13 NKJV

2. God initiated love toward us in choosing us to be his children.

﹏ The LORD did not choose you and lavish his love on you because you were larger or greater than other nations, for you were the smallest of all nations! It was simply because the LORD loves you, and because he was keeping the oath he had sworn to your ancestors. That is why the LORD rescued you with such amazing power from your slavery under Pharaoh in Egypt. Understand, therefore, that the LORD your God is indeed God. He is the faithful God who keeps his covenant for a thousand generations and constantly loves those who love him and obey his commands.

Deuteronomy 7:7–9 NLT

﹏ Long ago, even before he made the world, God loved us and chose us in Christ to be holy and without fault in his eyes. His unchanging plan has always been to adopt us into his own family by bringing us to himself through Jesus Christ. And this gave him great pleasure.

Ephesians 1:4–5 NLT

3. God demonstrated his love for us by sending Christ to die for undeserving sinners.

﹏ For God so loved the world, that he gave his only begotten Son, that whosoever believeth in him should not perish, but have everlasting life.

John 3:16

✦ But God commendeth his love toward us, in that, while we were yet sinners, Christ died for us.

Romans 5:8

✦ We know what real love is because Christ gave up his life for us.

1 John 3:16 NLT

4. God providentially works for good in the lives of those who love him.

✦ And we know that in all things God works for the good of those who love him, who have been called according to his purpose.

Romans 8:28 NIV

✦ The LORD watches over all who love him, but all the wicked he will destroy.

Psalm 145:20 NIV

✦ "The LORD your God in your midst, the Mighty One, will save; He will rejoice over you with gladness, He will quiet you in His love, He will rejoice over you with singing."

Zephaniah 3:17 NKJV

5. The Lord disciplines those whom he loves.

✦ My son, do not despise the LORD's discipline and do not resent his rebuke, because the LORD disciplines those he loves, as a father the son he delights in.

Proverbs 3:11–12 NIV

✦ For our earthly fathers disciplined us for a few years, doing the best they knew how. But God's discipline is always right and good for us because it means we will share in his holiness. No discipline is enjoyable while it is happening—it is painful! But afterward there will be a quiet harvest of right living for those who are trained in this way.

Hebrews 12:10–11 NLT

~ "As many as I love, I rebuke and chasten."

Revelation 3:19 NKJV

6. Our heavenly Father listens to the prayers of his children.

~ I love the LORD, because he hath heard my voice and my supplications. Because he hath inclined his ear unto me, therefore will I call upon him as long as I live.

Psalm 116:1–2

7. God loves those who are cheerful givers and good stewards of their possessions.

~ So let each one give as he purposes in his heart, not grudgingly or of necessity; for God loves a cheerful giver. And God is able to make all grace abound toward you, that you, always having all sufficiency in all things, may have an abundance for every good work.

2 Corinthians 9:7–8 NKJV

8. The Lord has prepared a future for us that exceeds our human capacity to anticipate.

~ "No eye has seen, no ear has heard, and no mind has imagined what God has prepared for those who love him."

1 Corinthians 2:9 NLT

9. God has promised the crown of life to those who love him.

~ Blessed is the man who endures temptation; for when he has been proved, he will receive the crown of life which the Lord has promised to those who love Him.

James 1:12 NKJV

10. Nothing can separate us from God's eternal love.

⊷ He who did not spare His own Son, but delivered Him up for us all, how shall He not with Him also freely give us all things? . . . Who shall separate us from the love of Christ? Shall tribulation, or distress, or persecution, or famine, or nakedness, or peril, or sword? . . . For I am persuaded that neither death nor life, nor angels nor principalities nor powers, nor things present nor things to come, nor height nor depth, nor any other created thing, shall be able to separate us from the love of God which is in Christ Jesus our Lord.

Romans 8:32, 35, 38–39 NKJV

Prayer

Father of love, I marvel at the love that you have lavished on the likes of me. To my dying day, the profoundest thought to grip my soul will always be the simple truth sung by the youngest of children, "Jesus loves me, this I know, for the Bible tells me so." To know that nothing in this world will ever be able to separate me from your love is my greatest comfort. I pray that your love will so radiate from my life that others may be drawn to you through me. I offer this prayer in the name of the one who loved me and gave himself for me.

Promise

For I am persuaded that neither death nor life, nor angels nor principalities nor powers, nor things present nor things to come, nor height nor depth, nor any other created thing, shall be able to separate us from the love of God which is in Christ Jesus our Lord.

Romans 8:38–39 NKJV

41

FACING OUR OWN DEATH

The worst thing that can happen to you is not the death of a loved one, a prolonged illness, or a painful accident. The worst thing that could happen to you would be to suffer for nothing, die, and be lost forever. God's people suffer for something—for Someone—and when they die, they enter into heaven where all their investment of suffering is transformed into glory.

—Warren W. Wiersbe, *Why Us?*

1. In the face of death we can take comfort in knowing that the grave is not the end of our existence.

I know the LORD is always with me. I will not be shaken, for he is right beside me. No wonder my heart is filled with joy, and my mouth shouts his praises! My body rests in safety. For you will not leave my soul among the dead or allow your godly one to rot in the grave. You will show me the way of life, granting me the joy of your presence and the pleasures of living with you forever.

Psalm 16:8–11 NLT

↬ Jesus said to her, "I am the resurrection and the life; he who believes in Me will live even if he dies; and everyone who lives and believes in Me will never die. Do you believe this?"

John 11:25–26 NASB

2. The length of our lives and timing of our deaths are in the hands of our sovereign Lord.

↬ "Do not be afraid. I am the First and the Last. I am the Living One; I was dead, and behold I am alive for ever and ever! And I hold the keys of death and Hades."

Revelation 1:17–18 NIV

3. As our bodies weaken and deteriorate, we can experience inner renewal as we focus on the unseen and eternal realities which are ours in Christ.

↬ Therefore we do not lose heart. Even though our outward man is perishing, yet the inward man is being renewed day by day. For our light affliction, which is but for a moment, is working for us a far more exceeding and eternal weight of glory, while we do not look at the things which are seen, but at the things which are not seen. For the things which are seen are temporary, but the things which are not seen are eternal. For we know that if our earthly house, this tent, is destroyed, we have a building from God, a house not made with hands, eternal in the heavens.

2 Corinthians 4:16–5:1 NKJV

↬ Our earthly bodies, which die and decay, will be different when they are resurrected, for they will never die. Our bodies now disappoint us, but when they are raised, they will be full of glory. They are weak now, but when they are raised, they will be full of power. They are natural human bodies now, but when they are raised, they will be spiritual bodies. For just as there are natural bodies, so also there are spiritual bodies.

1 Corinthians 15:42–44 NLT

43

✎ We expected to die. But as a result, we learned not to rely on ourselves, but on God who can raise the dead.

2 Corinthians 1:9 NLT

4. Physical death ushers believers into the presence of Christ, which is a far better state.

✎ For to me, living is for Christ, and dying is even better. Yet if I live, that means fruitful service for Christ. I really don't know which is better. I'm torn between two desires: Sometimes I want to live, and sometimes I long to go and be with Christ. That would be far better for me.

Philippians 1:21–23 NLT

5. Christ's death on our behalf enables us to overcome the fear of dying.

✎ Because God's children are human beings—made of flesh and blood—Jesus also became flesh and blood by being born in human form. For only as a human being could he die, and only by dying could he break the power of the Devil, who had the power of death. Only in this way could he deliver those who have lived all their lives as slaves to the fear of dying.

Hebrews 2:14–15 NLT

6. When facing death we can take comfort in the knowledge that nothing, including death itself, can separate us from the love of Christ.

✎ Yea, though I walk through the valley of the shadow of death, I will fear no evil: for thou art with me; thy rod and thy staff they comfort me.

Psalm 23:4

✎ Who shall separate us from the love of Christ? . . . For I am convinced that neither death nor life, neither angels nor demons, neither the present nor the future, nor any powers, neither height nor depth, nor anything else in all creation, will be able to separate us from the love of God that is in Christ Jesus our Lord.

Romans 8:35, 38–39 NIV

⁓ Precious in the sight of the LORD is the death of his saints.

Psalm 116:15 NIV

7. We can face death with the assurance that Christ has prepared a special dwelling place in the heavenly dimension into which he will welcome us.

⁓ "Do not let your heart be troubled; believe in God, believe also in Me. In My Father's house are many dwelling places; if it were not so, I would have told you; for I go to prepare a place for you. If I go and prepare a place for you, I will come again and receive you to Myself, that where I am, there you may be also."

John 14:1–3 NASB

8. At the end of our lives we can joyfully anticipate an eternity in Christ's presence, where we will no longer experience suffering, tears, or pain.

⁓ I heard a loud shout from the throne, saying, "Look, the home of God is now among his people! He will live with them, and they will be his people. God himself will be with them. He will remove all of their sorrows, and there will be no more death or sorrow or crying or pain. For the old world and its evils are gone forever."

Revelation 21:3–4 NLT

Prayer

Lord, I have just been dealt a crushing blow. The words "terminal illness" were words I had hoped never to hear. I have never felt so close to you and so far away at the same time. The prospect

45

of entering a new incredible world where tears and pain do not exist is welcome, but the thought of leaving behind those I hold dear envelops me in sorrow. I need your grace to bear what lies ahead and to prepare myself for heaven. My loved ones need your comfort desperately. Give me an accepting, expectant heart, Lord. Help me to trust you like a child and to realize that when I see my Savior face to face, it will be the happiest day of my life.

Promise

Who shall separate us from the love of Christ? . . . For I am convinced that neither death nor life, neither angels nor demons, neither the present nor the future, nor any powers, neither height nor depth, nor anything else in all creation, will be able to separate us from the love of God that is in Christ Jesus our Lord.

Romans 8:35, 38–39 NIV

FINANCIAL PERSPECTIVES

*The holy art of the child of God is so to possess the things
that are seen, that he can truly say that nothing on earth
delights him but his God . . . Never let it be said that he
who has God and God alone has nothing but God, for he
who has God, has in Him everything.*

—Abraham Kuyper, *To Be Near Unto God*

1. All wealth should be viewed as a gift from God.

When God gives any man wealth and possessions, and enables
him to enjoy them, to accept his lot and be happy in his work—
this is a gift of God.

Ecclesiastes 5:19 NIV

The blessing of the LORD makes a person rich.

Proverbs 10:22 NLT

The rich and the poor have this in common: The LORD made
them both.

Proverbs 22:2 NLT

2. Even in times of material scarcity, contentment should be a hallmark of our life in Christ.

↝ I have learned to be content in whatever circumstances I am. I know how to get along with humble means, and I also know how to live in prosperity; in any and every circumstance I have learned the secret of being filled and going hungry, both of having abundance and suffering need. I can do all things through Him who strengthens me.

Philippians 4:11–13 NASB

↝ Godliness with contentment is great gain. For we brought nothing into this world, and it is certain we can carry nothing out. And having food and clothing, with these we shall be content.

1 Timothy 6:6–8 NKJV

↝ Make sure that your character is free from the love of money, being content with what you have.

Hebrews 13:5 NASB

↝ "Beware! Don't be greedy for what you don't have. Real life is not measured by how much we own."

Luke 12:15 NLT

3. Riches can become a source of pride and self-confidence, drawing us away from the Lord.

↝ This is what the LORD says: "Let not the wise man gloat in his wisdom, or the mighty man in his might, or the rich man in his riches. Let them boast in this alone: that they truly know me and understand that I am the LORD who is just and righteous, whose love is unfailing, and that I delight in these things. I, the LORD, have spoken!"

Jeremiah 9:23–24 NLT

↝ For the love of money is a root of all kinds of evil. Some people, eager for money, have wandered from the faith and pierced themselves with many griefs.

1 Timothy 6:10 NIV

↝ "How hard it is for the rich to enter the kingdom of God. Indeed, it is easier for a camel to go through the eye of a needle than for a rich man to enter the kingdom of God."

Luke 18:25 NIV

4. God's infinite resources and power are adequate to meet our daily needs in times of financial difficulty.

↝ Give us this day our daily bread.

Matthew 6:11

↝ My God will meet all your needs according to his glorious riches in Christ Jesus.

Philippians 4:19 NIV

↝ "So do not worry, saying, 'What shall we eat?' or 'What shall we drink?' or 'What shall we wear?' For the pagans run after all these things, and your heavenly Father knows that you need them. But seek first his kingdom and his righteousness, and all these things will be given to you as well."

Matthew 6:31–33 NIV

5. It is impossible to give simultaneous allegiance to money and to the Lord.

↝ "No one can serve two masters. For you will hate one and love the other, or be devoted to one and despise the other. You cannot serve both God and money."

Luke 16:13 NLT

6. Generosity shown to those in need represents an investment in eternity.

↝ Tell those who are rich in this world not to be proud and not to trust in their money, which will soon be gone. But their trust should be in the living God, who richly gives us all we need for our enjoyment. Tell them to use their money to do good. They should be rich in good works and should give generously to those in need, always being ready to share with others whatever God has given them. By doing this they will be storing up their treasure as a good foundation for the future so that they may take hold of real life.

1 Timothy 6:17–19 NLT

Prayer

Lord, I need your perspective on all that is material. The world shouts at me that things make my life meaningful, but I know better. Remind me that my real treasure is eternal. Root from my heart those things that I cherish more than I cherish you. Create in me a desire to share with those in need out of the abundance with which I have been blessed. Enable me in the lean years to trust you with my welfare and the welfare of my family. This I pray in the name of my Savior who was rich, yet for my sake became poor.

Promise

My God will meet all your needs according to his glorious riches in Christ Jesus.

Philippians 4:19 NIV

FINDING PEACE

You will never have true peace until your mind is satisfied. If you merely get some emotional or psychological experience, it may keep you quiet and give you rest for a while, but sooner or later a problem will arise, a situation will confront you, a question will come to your mind, perhaps through reading a book, or in a conversation, and you will not be able to answer, and so you will lose your peace. There is no true peace with God until the mind has seen and grasped and taken hold of this blessed doctrine (justification), and so finds itself at rest

—Martyn Lloyd-Jones, *Romans: Exposition of Chapter 5*

1. The ultimate source of peace is Christ, the Prince of Peace.

For unto us a child is born, unto us a son is given: and the government shall be upon his shoulder: and his name shall be

51

called Wonderful, Counsellor, the mighty God, the everlasting Father, the Prince of Peace.

Isaiah 9:6

✦ Glory to God in the highest, and on earth peace, good will toward men.

Luke 2:14

✦ Let the peace of Christ rule in your hearts, since as members of one body you were called to peace.

Colossians 3:15 NIV

2. Peace becomes real in our hearts as we place our faith in Christ and experience justification before a holy God.

✦ Therefore, having been justified by faith, we have peace with God through our Lord Jesus Christ.

Romans 5:1 NKJV

✦ There is therefore now no condemnation to those who are in Christ Jesus, who do not walk according to the flesh, but according to the Spirit.

Romans 8:1 NKJV

✦ For he himself is our peace, who has made the two one and has destroyed the barrier, the dividing wall of hostility, by abolishing in his flesh the law with its commandments and regulations. His purpose was to create in himself one new man out of the two, thus making peace, and in this one body to reconcile both of them to God through the cross, by which he put to death their hostility. He came and preached peace to you who were far away and peace to those who were near. For through him we both have access to the Father by one Spirit.

Ephesians 2:14–18 NIV

✦ And, having made peace through the blood of his cross, by him to reconcile all things unto himself.

Colossians 1:20

✸ The chastisement of our peace was upon him.

Isaiah 53:5

3. Peace comes from the Lord as we share our concerns in prayer and reflect on his Word.

✸ Those who love your law have great peace and do not stumble.

Psalm 119:165 NLT

✸ Don't worry about anything; instead, pray about everything. Tell God what you need, and thank him for all he has done. If you do this, you will experience God's peace, which is far more wonderful than the human mind can understand. His peace will guard your hearts and minds as you live in Christ Jesus.

Philippians 4:6–7 NLT

✸ Now may the Lord of peace Himself give you peace always in every way. The Lord be with you all.

2 Thessalonians 3:16 NKJV

✸ "The LORD turn his face toward you and give you peace."

Numbers 6:26 NIV

4. Peace is a supernatural fruit of the Spirit's work in our lives and is distinct from what the world understands as the meaning of peace.

✸ The fruit of the Spirit is . . . peace.

Galatians 5:22

✸ The LORD will bless his people with peace.

Psalm 29:11

✸ "Peace I leave with you, My peace I give to you; not as the world gives do I give to you. Let not your heart be troubled, neither let it be afraid."

John 14:27 NKJV (see also 16:33)

↝ You will keep in perfect peace all who trust in you, whose thoughts are fixed on you!

Isaiah 26:3 NLT

5. Joy and good health frequently are by-products of God's peace.

↝ There is deceit in the hearts of those who plot evil, but joy for those who promote peace.

Proverbs 12:20 NIV

↝ A heart at peace gives life to the body, but envy rots the bones.

Proverbs 14:30 NIV

6. Once we have experienced Christ's peace in our hearts, it should be our desire to pursue peace in all of our relationships with others.

↝ Depart from evil, and do good; seek peace, and pursue it.

Psalm 34:14

↝ "Blessed are the peacemakers: for they shall be called the children of God."

Matthew 5:9

↝ Have peace one with another.

Mark 9:50

↝ Never pay back evil for evil to anyone. Do things in such a way that everyone can see you are honorable. Do your part to live in peace with everyone, as much as possible.

Romans 12:17–18 NLT (see also 14:19)

↝ Be of good comfort, be of one mind, live in peace; and the God of love and peace will be with you.

2 Corinthians 13:11 NKJV

↶ Be at peace among yourselves.

1 Thessalonians 5:13

↶ Follow peace with all men, and holiness, without which no man shall see the Lord.

Hebrews 12:14

↶ When a man's ways please the LORD, he maketh even his enemies to be at peace with him.

Proverbs 16:7

Prayer

O Lord, you know the circumstances in my life that leave me troubled and upset. At times the weight of that burden threatens to crush my trusting spirit. I ask for the faith to claim your peace in the face of unrelenting pressures. You have promised your perfect peace for those who keep their thoughts focused on you. Give me that singleness of vision that I may see you in the midst of my trials. Fill my heart now with the Holy Spirit's fruit of peace. May your peace guard and surround my heart and thoughts as I draw on your resources. This I pray through the name of Christ, the Prince of Peace.

Promise

For I am persuaded that neither death nor life, nor angels nor principalities nor powers, nor things present nor things to come, nor height nor depth, nor any other created thing, shall be able to separate us from the love of God which is in Christ Jesus our Lord.

Romans 8:38–39 NKJV

Fixing Our Eyes on the Lord

Being saved and seeing Jesus are not the same thing. Many
are partakers of God's grace who have never seen Jesus.
When once you have seen Jesus, you can never be the same;
other things do not appeal as they used to do.

—Oswald Chambers, *My Utmost for His Highest*

1. God the Father is not physically visible to our finite eyes.

⁓ "Please, show me Your glory." . . . But He said, "You cannot
see My face; for no man shall see Me, and live. . . . Then I will
take away My hand, and you shall see My back; but My face
shall not be seen."

Exodus 33:18, 20, 23 NKJV

⁓ No one has seen God at any time. The only begotten Son,
who is in the bosom of the Father, He has declared Him.

John 1:18 NKJV

2. The prophet Isaiah had the unique opportunity of seeing the glory of God. He experienced an overwhelming sense of his sinful unworthiness to gaze at the divine holy presence.

↝ In the year that King Uzziah died, I saw the Lord seated on a throne, high and exalted, and the train of his robe filled the temple. . . . "Woe to me!" I cried. "I am ruined! For I am a man of unclean lips, and I live among a people of unclean lips, and my eyes have seen the King, the LORD Almighty."

Isaiah 6:1, 5 NIV

3. In the first century, God chose to make himself visible through the incarnate body of Christ, the divine Son of God.

↝ And the Word was made flesh, and dwelt among us, (and we beheld his glory, the glory as of the only begotten of the Father,) full of grace and truth.

John 1:14

↝ But emptied Himself, taking the form of a bond-servant, and being made in the likeness of men. Being found in appearance as a man, He humbled Himself by becoming obedient to the point of death, even death on a cross.

Philippians 2:7–8 NASB

↝ Philip said to Him, "Lord, show us the Father, and it is enough for us." Jesus said to him, "Have I been so long with you, and yet you have not come to know Me, Philip? He who has seen Me has seen the Father; how can you say, 'Show us the Father?'"

John 14:8–9 NASB

4. On rare occasions, Christ's disciples were allowed to gaze on the glory of his divine presence.

57

↜ A bright cloud came over them, and a voice from the cloud said, "This is my beloved Son, and I am fully pleased with him. Listen to him." The disciples were terrified and fell face down on the ground. Jesus came over and touched them. "Get up," he said, "don't be afraid." And when they looked, they saw only Jesus with them.

Matthew 17:5–8 NLT

↜ As they sat down to eat, he took a small loaf of bread, asked God's blessing on it, broke it, then gave it to them. Suddenly, their eyes were opened, and they recognized him. And at that moment he disappeared!

Luke 24:30–31 NLT

5. At his promised return, Christ will be physically visible.

↜ Behold, he cometh with clouds; and every eye shall see him.

Revelation 1:7

↜ The throne of God and of the Lamb shall be in [the city]; and his servants shall serve him. And they shall see his face; and his name will be on their foreheads.

Revelation 22:3–4

↜ Yes, dear friends, we are already God's children, and we can't even imagine what we will be like when Christ returns. But we do know that when he comes we will be like him, for we will see him as he really is. And all who believe this will keep themselves pure, just as Christ is pure.

1 John 3:2–3 NLT

6. Christ allows us in our earthly state to see him with the eyes of faith.

↜ Blessed are the pure in heart: for they shall see God.

Matthew 5:8

↬ Jesus said to him, "Thomas, because you have seen Me, you have believed. Blessed are those who have not seen and yet have believed."

John 20:29 NKJV

↬ We look not at the things which are seen, but at the things which are not seen; for the things which are seen are temporal, but the things which are not seen are eternal.

2 Corinthians 4:18 NASB

7. Distractions in the world around us can hinder us from maintaining a God-centered focus.

↬ Peter said to Him, "Lord, if it is You, command me to come to You on the water." And He said, "Come!" And Peter got out of the boat and walked on the water and came toward Jesus. But seeing the wind, he became frightened, and beginning to sink, he cried out, "Lord save me!" Immediately Jesus stretched out His hand and took hold of him, and said to him, "O you of little faith, why did you doubt?"

Matthew 14:28–31 NASB

↬ "The eye is the lamp of the body. If your eyes are good, your whole body will be full of light. But if your eyes are bad, your whole body will be full of darkness. If then the light within you is darkness, how great is that darkness! No one can serve two masters. Either he will hate the one and love the other, or he will be devoted to the one and despise the other. You cannot serve both God and Money."

Matthew 6:22–24 NIV

↬ "But the worries of the world, and the deceitfulness of riches, and the desires for other things enter in and choke the word, and it becomes unfruitful."

Mark 4:19 NASB

↬ Since you have been raised to new life with Christ, set your sights on the realities of heaven, where Christ sits at God's right hand in the place of honor and power. Let heaven fill your thoughts. Do not think only about things down here on earth. For you died when Christ died, and your real life is hidden with Christ in God. And when Christ, who is your real life, is revealed to the whole world, you will share in all his glory.

Colossians 3:1–4 NLT

8. As we run the race of life before the watching eyes of a heavenly audience, we must fix our eyes on Jesus.

⟶ Therefore, since we are surrounded by such a huge crowd of witnesses to the life of faith, let us strip off every weight that slows us down, especially the sin that so easily hinders our progress. And let us run with endurance the race that God has set before us. We do this by keeping our eyes on Jesus, on whom our faith depends from start to finish. He was willing to die a shameful death on the cross because of the joy he knew would be his afterward. Now he is seated in the place of highest honor beside God's throne in heaven.

Hebrews 12:1–2 NLT

⟶ My eyes are ever on the LORD.

Psalm 25:15 NIV

Prayer

Dear Father who sees all, I need to see only you. My eternal focus is in need of sharpening. The distractions of this world have dulled my spiritual eyesight. Give me tunnel vision, Lord, that others, seeing me, will see only you.

Promise

Blessed are the pure in heart: for they shall see God.

Matthew 5:8

GIVING THANKS IN ALL CIRCUMSTANCES

Sometimes I go to God and say, "God, if Thou dost never answer another prayer while I live on this earth, I will still worship Thee as long as I live and in the ages to come for what Thou hast done already." God's already put me so far in debt that if I were to live one million millenniums, I couldn't pay Him for what He's done for me.

—A. W. Tozer, *Worship, the Missing Jewel*

1. The absence of thanksgiving in one's life is a mark of a heart that has grown cold.

⇥ Although they knew God, they did not glorify Him as God, nor were thankful, but became futile in their thoughts, and their foolish hearts were darkened.

Romans 1:21 NKJV

61

⁊⁊ But realize this, that in the last days difficult times will come. For men will be lovers of self, lovers of money, boastful, arrogant, revilers, disobedient to parents, ungrateful. . . .

2 Timothy 3:1–2 NASB

2. Awareness of the acts and attributes of God should generate a spirit of thankfulness.

⁊⁊ Sing praise to the LORD, you His godly ones, and give thanks to His holy name.

Psalm 30:4 NASB

⁊⁊ Praise the LORD! Oh give thanks to the LORD, for He is good; for His lovingkindness is everlasting.

Psalm 106:1 NASB

⁊⁊ At midnight I shall rise to give thanks to You, because of Your righteous ordinances.

Psalm 119:62 NASB

3. God's provision of food for our physical nourishment is an ongoing cause for thankfulness.

⁊⁊ Then he took the seven loaves and the fish, and when he had given thanks, he broke them and gave them to the disciples, and they in turn to the people.

Matthew 15:36 NIV

⁊⁊ When he had taken the seven loaves and given thanks, he broke them and gave them to his disciples to set before the people, and they did so. They had a few small fish as well; he gave thanks for them also and told the disciples to distribute them.

Mark 8:6–7 NIV

⁊⁊ When he was at the table with them, he took bread, gave thanks, broke it and began to give it to them. Then their eyes were opened and they recognized him, and he disappeared from their sight.

Luke 24:30–31 NIV

All eyes look to you for help; you give them their food as they need it. When you open your hand, you satisfy the hunger and thirst of every living thing.

Psalm 145:15–16 NLT

4. Thanksgiving should be a regular part of our corporate worship.

I will give You thanks in the great assembly; I will praise You among many people.

Psalm 35:18 NKJV

Let us come before His presence with thanksgiving; let us shout joyfully to Him with psalms.

Psalm 95:2 NKJV

Enter his gates with thanksgiving; go into his courts with praise. Give thanks to him and bless his name.

Psalm 100:4 NLT

"Amen! Blessing and glory and wisdom and thanksgiving and honor and power and strength belong to our God forever and forever. Amen!"

Revelation 7:12 NLT

5. Thanksgiving can be an antidote to destructive worry and anxiety.

Do not be anxious about anything, but in everything, by prayer and petition, with thanksgiving, present your requests to God. And the peace of God, which transcends all understanding, will guard your hearts and your minds in Christ Jesus.

Philippians 4:6 NIV

63

6. In all the ups and downs of life, we should maintain an attitude of thankfulness to the Lord.

~ In everything give thanks; for this is God's will for you in Christ Jesus.

1 Thessalonians 5:18 NASB

~ Always giving thanks for all things in the name of our Lord Jesus Christ to God, even the Father.

Ephesians 5:20 NASB

~ And let the peace that comes from Christ rule in your hearts. For as members of one body you are all called to live in peace. And always be thankful. . . . And whatever you do or say, let it be as a representative of the Lord Jesus, all the while giving thanks through him to God the Father.

Colossians 3:15, 17 NLT

7. Our answered prayers on behalf of others can be the cause of many giving thanks to God.

~ He will rescue us because you are helping by praying for us. As a result, many will give thanks to God because so many people's prayers for our safety have been answered.

2 Corinthians 1:11 NLT

Prayer

Lord, the psalmist put it well, "My cup overflows." Some days I feel as if I will explode if I cannot express the thanksgiving that is welling up inside me. Thank you for the incomparable joy that is mine because I am your child forever.

To be honest, there are other days, Lord, when words of thanksgiving do not spill so easily from my lips. Enable me in those times to thank you because you have promised to walk with me through the furnace of affliction. Thank you for working your skillful purpose in my life in sickness and in health, in plenty and in want, in joy and in sorrow.

Promise

Do not be anxious about anything, but in everything, by prayer and petition, with thanksgiving, present your requests to God. And the peace of God, which transcends all understanding, will guard your hearts and your minds in Christ Jesus.

Philippians 4:6 NIV

GRANTING FORGIVENESS

*I am telling you what Christianity is. I did not invent it.
And there, right in the middle of it, I find "Forgive us our
sins as we forgive those that sin against us." There is no
slightest suggestion that we are offered forgiveness on any
other terms. It is made perfectly clear that if we do not forgive we shall not be forgiven. There are no two ways about
it. What are we to do?*

—C. S. Lewis, *Mere Christianity*

**1. The foundation for all forgiveness is the sacrificial
and substitutionary death of Christ for sinners. Without
this work of Christ we would have no hope for forgiveness.**

↞ So we praise God for the wonderful kindness he has poured
out on us because we belong to his dearly loved Son. He is so
rich in kindness that he purchased our freedom through the
blood of his Son, and our sins are forgiven.

Ephesians 1:6–7 NLT

⚘ He has delivered us from the power of darkness and translated us into the kingdom of the Son of His love, in whom we have redemption through His blood, the forgiveness of sins.

Colossians 1:13–14 NKJV

⚘ Without the shedding of blood, there is no forgiveness of sins.

Hebrews 9:22 NLT

2. Confession is the necessary link between our sin and forgiveness. Scripture encourages us to confess our sins to God and resist the temptation to cover over those sins.

⚘ When I kept silent, my bones wasted away through my groaning all day long. For day and night your hand was heavy upon me; my strength was sapped as in the heat of summer. Then I acknowledged my sin to you and did not cover up my iniquity. I said, "I will confess my transgressions to the LORD"—and you forgave the guilt of my sin.

Psalm 32:3–5 NIV

⚘ If we say that we have no sin, we deceive ourselves, and the truth is not in us. If we confess our sins, He is faithful and just to forgive us our sins and to cleanse us from all unrighteousness.

1 John 1:8–9 NKJV

3. When others have been wronged by our sinful behavior, it is important that we confess our sin to these individuals as well as to God.

⚘ Confess your sins to one another, and pray for one another, so that you may be healed.

James 5:16 NASB

⚘ Be kind to one another, tender-hearted, forgiving each other, just as God in Christ also has forgiven you.

Ephesians 4:32 NASB

67

↬ Bearing with one another, and forgiving each other, whoever has a complaint against anyone; just as the Lord forgave you, so also should you.

Colossians 3:13 NASB

4. Genuine repentance calls for a change of attitudes and actions in the one who has sinned.

↬ For God can use sorrow in our lives to help us turn away from sin and seek salvation. We will never regret that kind of sorrow. But sorrow without repentance is the kind that results in death. Just see what this godly sorrow produced in you! Such earnestness, such concern to clear yourselves, such indignation, such alarm, such longing to see me, such zeal, and such a readiness to punish the wrongdoer. You showed that you have done everything you could to make things right.

2 Corinthians 7:10–11 NLT

↬ "Produce fruit in keeping with repentance."

Matthew 3:8 NIV

5. God expects us to grant forgiveness to those who profess to have repented of their sins. We do not need to wait until we see evidence of the fruit of repentance in their lives.

↬ "If your brother sins against you, rebuke him; and if he repents, forgive him. And if he sins against you seven times in a day and seven times in a day returns to you, saying, 'I repent,' you shall forgive him."

Luke 17:3–4 NKJV

6. Once we have received God's forgiveness for our sins, we are promised that God will not continue to "think" on them. The sins of our past are fully forgiven and will not be held against us.

ᴧ "I will forgive their wickedness and will never again remember their sins."

Jeremiah 31:34 NLT

ᴧ "I—yes, I alone—am the one who blots out your sins for my own sake and will never think of them again."

Isaiah 43:25 NLT

7. If we have received Christ's forgiveness, we in turn must be willing to forgive others who have sinned against us.

ᴧ Be kind and compassionate to one another, forgiving each other, just as in Christ God forgave you.

Ephesians 4:32 NIV (see also Col. 3:13)

ᴧ "And forgive us our debts, as we forgive our debtors."

Matthew 6:12 NKJV

ᴧ "I do not say to you, up to seven times, but up to seventy times seven. . . . 'You wicked servant! I forgave you all that debt because you begged me. Should you not also have had compassion on your fellow servant, just as I had pity on you?' And his master was angry, and delivered him to the torturers until he should pay all that was due to him. So My heavenly Father also will do to you if each of you, from his heart, does not forgive his brother his trespasses."

Matthew 18:22, 32–35 NKJV

8. Scripture provides models of forgiveness. The prime motivating example is that of Christ at his crucifixion.

ᴧ But Jesus was saying, "Father, forgive them; for they do not know what they are doing."

Luke 23:34 NASB

ᴧ They went on stoning Stephen as he called on the Lord and said, "Lord Jesus, receive my spirit!" Then falling on his knees, he cried out with a loud voice, "Lord, do not hold this sin against them!" Having said this, he fell asleep.

Acts 7:59–60 NASB

Prayer

Father, how often I have needed to return, as the prodigal son returned, to receive your forgiveness and the forgiveness of others. Your forgiveness in my life has been a miracle of grace. Yet somehow it remains difficult for me to forgive those who have wronged me deeply. There is a sinful part of me that wants to hang on to the hurt and never let go. Lord, I pray that your Holy Spirit would transform my willfully stubborn heart and create in me a desire to forgive freely, as I have been forgiven. Thank you that the well of your mercy never runs dry.

Promise

"I—yes, I alone—am the one who blots out your sins for my own sake and will never think of them again."

Isaiah 43:25 NLT

GRIEVING THE DEATH OF SOMEONE CLOSE

Death wounds us, but wounds are meant to heal. And—
given time—they will. But we must want to be healed. We
cannot be like the child who keeps picking the scab from a
cut. Life must move forward, even though we may have lost
the one who was the dearest to us, even though meaning
seems to have been removed from living.

—Joseph Bayly, *The View from a Hearse*

1. Christ, who experienced firsthand the pain of losing someone close to him, offers his comfort and grace to us as we grieve the loss of our loved one.

↗ Jesus wept. Then the Jews said, "See how He loved him."

John 11:35–36 NKJV

↗ A man of sorrows and acquainted with grief.

Isaiah 53:3 NASB

✝ For we do not have a high priest who is unable to sympathize with our weaknesses.

Hebrews 4:15 NIV

✝ "Come to Me, all you who labor and are heavy laden, and I will give you rest."

Matthew 11:28 NKJV

2. Christians who mourn the death of fellow believers need not experience the despairing and hopeless grief of those who live without Christ.

✝ Brothers and sisters, I want you to know what will happen to the Christians who have died so you will not be full of sorrow like people who have no hope.

1 Thessalonians 4:13 NLT

3. Physical death ushers believers into the presence of Christ, which is a far better state.

✝ For to me, living is for Christ, and dying is even better. Yet if I live, that means fruitful service for Christ. I really don't know which is better. I'm torn between two desires: Sometimes I want to live, and sometimes I long to go and be with Christ. That would be far better for me.

Philippians 1:21–23 NLT

✝ Blessed are those who die in the Lord from now on. Yes, says the Spirit, they are blessed indeed, for they will rest from all their toils and trials; for their good deeds follow them!

Revelation 14:13 NLT

4. Death cannot separate us from the love of Christ.

*Yea, though I walk through the valley of the shadow of death, I will fear no evil: for thou art with me; thy rod and thy staff they comfort me.

Psalm 23:4

*Who shall separate us from the love of Christ? . . . For I am convinced that neither death nor life, neither angels nor demons, neither the present nor the future, nor any powers, neither height nor depth, nor anything else in all creation, will be able to separate us from the love of God that is in Christ Jesus our Lord.

Romans 8:35, 38–39 NIV

*I know the LORD is always with me. I will not be shaken, for he is right beside me. No wonder my heart is filled with joy, and my mouth shouts his praises! My body rests in safety. For you will not leave my soul among the dead or allow your godly one to rot in the grave. You will show me the way of life, granting me the joy of your presence and the pleasures of living with you forever.

Psalm 16:8–11 NLT

5. God has prepared a special dwelling place in the heavenly dimension into which he will welcome all who have died in Christ.

*"Do not let your heart be troubled; believe in God, believe also in Me. In My Father's house are many dwelling places; if it were not so, I would have told you; for I go to prepare a place for you. If I go and prepare a place for you, I will come again, and receive you to Myself, that where I am, there you may be also."

John 14:1–3 NASB

6. Our believing loved ones are enjoying an eternity in Christ's presence, where they will no longer experience suffering, tears, or pain.

73

✦ I heard a loud shout from the throne, saying, "Look, the home of God is now among his people! He will live with them, and they will be his people. God himself will be with them. He will remove all of their sorrows, and there will be no more death or sorrow or crying or pain. For the old world and its evils are gone forever."

Revelation 21:3–4 NLT

7. We know that death is not the end of our existence because we are promised a future bodily resurrection.

✦ Jesus said to her, "I am the resurrection and the life; he who believes in Me will live even if he dies; and everyone who lives and believes in Me will never die. Do you believe this?"

John 11:25–26 NASB

✦ Our earthly bodies, which die and decay, will be different when they are resurrected, for they will never die. Our bodies now disappoint us, but when they are raised, they will be full of glory. They are weak now, but when they are raised, they will be full of power. They are natural human bodies now, but when they are raised, they will be spiritual bodies. For just as there are natural bodies, so also there are spiritual bodies.

1 Corinthians 15:42–44 NLT

8. We can expect that Christ's second coming will include a reunion with loved ones who have died in Christ.

✦ For since we believe that Jesus died and was raised to life again, we also believe that when Jesus comes, God will bring back with Jesus all the Christians who have died. I can tell you this directly from the Lord: We who are still living when the Lord returns will not rise to meet him ahead of those who are in their graves. For the Lord himself will come down from heaven with a commanding shout, with the call of the archangel, and with the trumpet call of God. First, all the Christians who have died will rise from their graves. Then, together with them, we who are still alive and remain on the earth will be caught up in the clouds to meet the Lord in the air and remain with him forever. So comfort and encourage each other with these words.

1 Thessalonians 4:14–18 NLT

9. The Lord himself comforts us and enables us to go on when we are grieving the loss of a loved one.

↬ All praise to the God and Father of our Lord Jesus Christ. He is the source of every mercy and the God who comforts us. He comforts us in all our troubles so that we can comfort others. When others are troubled, we will be able to give them the same comfort God has given us.

2 Corinthians 1:3–4 NLT

↬ Why do you say, O Jacob, and speak, O Israel: "My way is hidden from the LORD, and my just claim is passed over by my God"? Have you not known? Have you not heard? The everlasting God, the LORD, the Creator of the ends of the earth, neither faints nor is weary. There is no searching of His understanding. He gives power to the weak, and to those who have no might He increases strength.

Isaiah 40:27–29 NKJV

↬ Cast your burden on the LORD, and He shall sustain you.

Psalm 55:22 NKJV

↬ After you have suffered for a little while, the God of all grace, who called you to His eternal glory in Christ, will Himself perfect, confirm, strengthen and establish you.

1 Peter 5:10 NASB

Prayer

I'm not a Stoic, Lord. The truth is I'm reeling from my loss. Surely no one else has ever grieved as I am grieving now. My heart can only be described as an aching vacuum. If only I could be temporarily anesthetized.

75

I do not pretend to understand why someone so precious has been taken away, but I pray that in my grieving you would draw me to yourself. You are the only one who can lift me from the sinkhole of self-pity and help me to face the reality of my loss. In the absence of my loved one, may the blessed presence of your Spirit comfort me. I offer my loneliness to you knowing full well that you will never desert me. Enable me to rest in the knowledge that my future is in your wise and loving hands.

Promise

"I am the resurrection and the life; he who believes in Me will live even if he dies; and everyone who lives and believes in Me will never die."

John 11:25 NASB

GROWING OLDER

I do not want to be a grumpy old man. God threatens terrible things for those who grumble (Psalm 106:25–26). Murmuring dishonors the God who promises to work all things together for our good (Romans 8:28). Complaining puts out the light of our Christian witness (Philippians 2:14–15). A critical anxious spirit dries up our joy and peace (Philippians 4:6–7). That is not the way I want to grow old. I want to be like the aging man in Psalm 71.

—John Piper, *A Godward Life*

1. The ageless and eternal Triune God possesses none of the temporal limitations that we experience.

⁊ LORD, You have been our dwelling place in all generations. Before the mountains were brought forth, or ever You had formed the earth and the world, even from everlasting to everlasting, You are God.

Psalm 90:1–2 NKJV

↬ Thy throne, O God, is for ever and ever.

Hebrews 1:8

↬ "Lord, in the beginning you laid the foundation of the earth, and the heavens are the work of your hands. Even they will perish, but you remain forever. They will wear out like old clothing. You will roll them up like an old coat. They will fade away like old clothing. But you are always the same; you will never grow old."

Hebrews 1:10–12 NLT

↬ I am Alpha and Omega, the beginning and the end, the first and the last.

Revelation 22:13

2. The fact that life passes quickly is no surprise. Scripture uses several analogies from the physical world to illustrate the brevity of life.

↬ "Behold, You have made my days as handbreadths, and my lifetime as nothing in Your sight; surely every man at his best is a mere breath."

Psalm 39:5 NASB

↬ For a thousand years in your sight are like a day that has just gone by, or like a watch in the night. You sweep men away in the sleep of death; they are like the new grass of the morning— though in the morning it springs up new, by evening it is dry and withered.

Psalm 90:4–6 NIV

↬ "All flesh is grass, and all its loveliness is like the flower of the field. The grass withers, the flower fades, because the breath of the LORD blows upon it; surely the people are grass. The grass withers, the flower fades, but the word of our God stands forever."

Isaiah 40:6b–8 NKJV

↬ Look here, you people who say, "Today or tomorrow we are going to a certain town and will stay there a year. We will do business there and make a profit." How do you know what will happen tomorrow? For your life is like the morning fog—it's here a little while, then it's gone. What you ought to say is, "If the Lord wants us to, we will live and do this or that."

James 4:13–15 NLT

3. Life is here today and gone tomorrow. To invest our lives in eternity is good stewardship.

↬ And let the beauty of the LORD our God be upon us, and establish the work of our hands for us; yes, establish the work of our hands.

Psalm 90:17 NKJV

↬ So be careful how you live, not as fools but as those who are wise. Make the most of every opportunity for doing good in these evil days. Don't act thoughtlessly, but try to understand what the Lord wants you to do.

Ephesians 5:15–17 NLT

4. Fear of death has no place in the hearts of believers.

↬ The length of our days is seventy years—or eighty, if we have the strength; yet their span is but trouble and sorrow, for they quickly pass, and we fly away.

Psalm 90:10 NIV

↬ "Do not be afraid; I am the First and the Last. I am He who lives, and was dead, and behold, I am alive forevermore. Amen. And I have the keys of Hades and of Death."

Revelation 1:17b–18 NKJV

↬ "And who of you by being worried can add a single hour to his life?"

Matthew 6:27 NASB

5. The wisdom of the elderly is to be valued and respected.

79

↠ With the ancient is wisdom; and in length of days understanding.

Job 12:12

↠ The glory of young men is their strength, and the splendor of old men is their gray head.

Proverbs 20:29 NKJV

↠ Listen to your father who begot you, and do not despise your mother when she is old.

Proverbs 23:22 NKJV

6. Children and grandchildren are gifts from God to be enjoyed in one's older years. Likewise, children are blessed by the faith of those who have gone before them.

↠ Grandchildren are the crowning glory of the aged; parents are the pride of their children.

Proverbs 17:6 NLT

7. God expects us to pass the torch of faith from one generation to the next. This responsibility begins when our children are young.

↠ Train up a child in the way he should go, and when he is old he will not depart from it.

Proverbs 22:6 NKJV

↠ Even when I am old and gray, do not forsake me, O God, till I declare your power to the next generation, your might to all who are to come.

Psalm 71:18 NIV

↠ One generation will commend your works to another; they will tell of your mighty acts.

Psalm 145:4 NIV

↝ For I am mindful of the sincere faith within you, which first dwelt in your grandmother Lois, and your mother Eunice, and I am sure that it is in you as well.

2 Timothy 1:5 NASB

8. The Lord makes it possible to be productive in old age.

↝ But the godly will flourish like palm trees and grow strong like the cedars of Lebanon. For they are transplanted into the LORD's own house. They flourish in the courts of our God. Even in old age they will still produce fruit; they will remain vital and green.

Psalm 92:12–14 NLT

9. The Lord's care knows no age limits.

↝ Do not cast me away when I am old; do not forsake me when my strength is gone. . . . Since my youth, O God, you have taught me, and to this day I declare your marvelous deeds. Even when I am old and gray, do not forsake me, O God.

Psalm 71:9, 17–18 NIV

↝ Who satisfies your years with good things, so that your youth is renewed like the eagle.

Psalm 103:5 NASB

↝ Even to your old age I will be the same, and even to your graying years I will bear you! I have done it, and I will carry you; and I will bear you and I will deliver you.

Isaiah 46:4 NASB

Prayer

Everlasting, eternal Father, I am increasingly able to understand that life is but a breath. To look in the mirror is to be reminded that I am like the grass that withers and the flowers that fade. Help me to live each remaining day of my life looking forward to

81

the day when I shall be forever in your presence. Enable me to pass to the next generation the torch of faith that has sustained me in this life. Even as my strength wanes, help me to receive each new day as a gift from you. Help me to rest in the promise that you never forsake your own. This I pray in the name of Christ who is the Alpha and Omega, the beginning and the ending.

Promise

But the godly will flourish like palm trees and grow strong like the cedars of Lebanon. For they are transplanted into the LORD's own house. They flourish in the courts of our God. Even in old age they will still produce fruit; they will remain vital and green.

Psalm 92:12–14 NLT

HEAVENLY PERSPECTIVES

To be heavenly minded means to live a life of faith in things not seen (Hebrews 11:1). It means to live for the world to come, not this present world. It means to see all of life from an eternal perspective. It means to live every day and weigh every decision in the light of eternity. It means to live for that which is timeless, *not temporal; to live for that which is* spiritual, *not tangible; to live for that which is* invisible, *not visible. In short, the one who is heavenly minded has one overwhelming passion in life—God!*

—Steve Lawson, *Heaven Help Us*

1. The anticipation of heaven should occupy and preoccupy our thoughts in this present life.

Set your hearts on things above, where Christ is seated at the right hand of God. Set your minds on things above, not on earthly things.

Colossians 3:1–2 NIV

2. Heaven is a place of sinlessness.

↝ And nothing unclean . . . shall ever come into it.

Revelation 21:27 NASB

3. Heaven is a place of physical well-being.

↝ No one living in Zion will say, "I am ill"; and the sins of those who dwell there will be forgiven.

Isaiah 33:24 NIV

↝ He will remove all of their sorrows, and there will be no more . . . pain. For the old world and its evils are gone forever.

Revelation 21:4 NLT

4. Heaven is a place where death and sorrow do not exist.

↝ He will swallow up death for all time, and the Lord GOD will wipe tears away from all faces.

Isaiah 25:8 NASB

↝ "Death has been swallowed up in victory."

1 Corinthians 15:54 NIV

↝ Christ Jesus, our Savior, who broke the power of death and showed us the way to everlasting life through the Good News.

2 Timothy 1:10 NLT

↝ He will wipe every tear from their eyes. There will be no more death or mourning or crying or pain, for the old order of things has passed away.

Revelation 21:4 NIV

5. Heaven is a place of perfect knowledge.

↝ Now we see but a poor reflection as in a mirror; then we shall see face to face. Now I know in part; then I shall know fully, even as I am fully known.

1 Corinthians 13:12 NIV

✙ "No eye has seen, no ear has heard, and no mind has imagined what God has prepared for those who love him."

1 Corinthians 2:9 NLT

6. Heaven is a place of eternal joy and celebration.

✙ You will show me the path of life; in Your presence is fullness of joy; at Your right hand are pleasures forevermore.

Psalm 16:11 NKJV

✙ With everlasting joy on their heads. They shall obtain joy and gladness, and sorrow and sighing shall flee away.

Isaiah 35:10 NKJV

✙ He will wipe every tear from their eyes. There will be no more . . . mourning or crying.

Revelation 21:4 NIV

7. Heaven is a place where our deepest thirsts will be quenched.

✙ "To him who is thirsty I will give to drink without cost from the spring of the water of life."

Revelation 21:6 NIV

✙ And the angel showed me a pure river with the water of life, clear as crystal, flowing from the throne of God and of the Lamb, coursing down the center of the main street. On each side of the river grew a tree of life, bearing twelve crops of fruit.

Revelation 22:1–2 NLT

8. Heaven is a place where all legitimate needs are satisfied.

✙ "Never again will they hunger; never again will they thirst. The sun will not beat upon them, nor any scorching heat. For the

85

Lamb at the center of the throne will be their shepherd; he will lead them to springs of living water. And God will wipe away every tear from their eyes."

Revelation 7:16–17 NIV

9. Heaven is a place of intimate fellowship with God and Christ.

↜ "And if I go and prepare a place for you, I will come again and receive you to Myself; that where I am, there you may be also."

John 14:3 NKJV

↜ "Father, I desire that they also, whom You have given Me, be with Me where I am, so that they may see My glory which You have given Me, for You loved Me before the foundation of the world."

John 17:24 NASB

↜ We will be with the Lord forever.

1 Thessalonians 4:17

Prayer

Father in heaven, I ask you to create in me a desire to focus my thoughts on the life to come. I confess how easy it is to be enticed by the earthly, material world that surrounds me to the neglect of heavenly realities. I long to be more heavenly minded. Thank you for what you are now preparing for me in heaven. Thank you for the assurance that heaven is a place of eternal joy where death and sorrow do not exist. Prepare me in this life for my future heavenly home, where I will enjoy fellowship with you forever. This I pray through Christ who will one day welcome me into his heaven.

Promise

He will wipe every tear from their eyes. There will be no more death or mourning or crying or pain, for the old order of things has passed away.

Revelation 21:4 NIV

HONESTY

To be honest, as this world goes, is to be one man picked out of ten thousand.

—William Shakespeare, *Hamlet*

1. Honesty in speech, actions, and conduct is an essential part of God's moral law for people in all generations.

➤ "You shall not steal. You shall not bear false witness against your neighbor."

Exodus 20:15–16 NASB

➤ "You shall not steal, nor deal falsely, nor lie to one another."

Leviticus 19:11 NASB

2. The Lord despises the practice of acquiring financial gain through dishonesty.

➤ "But now I clap my hands in indignation over your dishonest gain and bloodshed. . . . Your princes plot conspiracies just as lions stalk their prey. They devour innocent people, seizing treasures and extorting wealth. They increase the number of widows in the land. . . . Your leaders are like wolves, who tear apart their victims. They actually destroy people's lives for profit!"

Ezekiel 22:13, 25, 27 NLT

⤞ The LORD abhors dishonest scales, but accurate weights are his delight.

Proverbs 11:1 NIV

3. The Lord delights to reward those who are honest in their conduct.

⤞ The ones who can live here are honest and fair, who reject making a profit by fraud, who stay far away from bribes, who refuse to listen to those who plot murder, who shut their eyes to all enticement to do wrong. These are the ones who will dwell on high. The rocks of the mountains will be their fortress of safety. Food will be supplied to them, and they will have water in abundance.

Isaiah 33:15–16 NLT

⤞ "You shall not have in your bag differing weights, a heavy and a light. You shall not have in your house differing measures, a large and a small. You shall have a perfect and just weight, a perfect and just measure, that your days may be lengthened in the land which the LORD your God is giving you."

Deuteronomy 25:13–15 NKJV

⤞ Look at those who are honest and good, for a wonderful future lies before those who love peace.

Psalm 37:37 NLT

4. Our business dealings should always be marked by honesty.

⤞ "Do not use dishonest standards when measuring length, weight or quantity. Use honest scales and honest weights, an honest ephah and an honest hin. I am the LORD your God, who brought you out of Egypt."

Leviticus 19:35–36 NIV

⚕ "If you sell land to one of your countrymen or buy any from him, do not take advantage of each other."

Leviticus 25:14 NIV

⚕ Honest scales and balances are from the LORD; all the weights in the bag are of his making.

Proverbs 16:11 NIV

⚕ The wicked borrows and does not pay back, but the righteous is gracious and gives.

Psalm 37:21 NASB

⚕ Jacob modeled honesty in returning money that didn't belong to him which had been placed in his sack.

Genesis 42–43

5. Honesty is noticed and valued when others see it practiced in our lives.

⚕ Kings take pleasure in honest lips; they value a man who speaks the truth.

Proverbs 16:13 NIV

⚕ We have regard for what is honorable, not only in the sight of the Lord, but also in the sight of men.

2 Corinthians 8:21 NASB

⚕ Be careful how you live among your unbelieving neighbors. Even if they accuse you of doing wrong, they will see your honorable behavior, and they will believe and give honor to God when he comes to judge the world.

1 Peter 2:12 NLT

6. Honesty in speech should be part of our new nature in Christ.

↦ Don't lie to each other, for you have stripped off your old evil nature and all its wicked deeds. In its place you have clothed yourselves with a brand-new nature that is continually being renewed as you learn more and more about Christ, who created this new nature within you.

Colossians 3:9–10 NLT

↦ A truthful witness gives honest testimony, but a false witness tells lies.

Proverbs 12:17 NIV

7. God's will is that we provide for ourselves and for those in need by honest work.

↦ If you are a thief, stop stealing. Begin using your hands for honest work, and then give generously to others in need.

Ephesians 4:28 NLT

8. The cultivation of patterns of honesty in place of dishonesty is encouraged through regular feeding on Scripture.

↦ Therefore, laying aside all malice, all guile, hypocrisy, envy, and all evil speaking, as newborn babes, desire the pure milk of the word, that you may grow thereby.

1 Peter 2:1–2 NKJV

9. When treated dishonestly, we should resist the impulse to seek revenge or be dishonest in return.

↦ So if you are suffering according to God's will, keep on doing what is right, and trust yourself to the God who made you, for he will never fail you.

1 Peter 4:19 NLT

↦ Do not repay anyone evil for evil. Be careful to do what is right in the eyes of everybody. . . . Do not take revenge, my friends, but leave room for God's wrath, for it is written: "It is mine to avenge; I will repay," says the Lord. . . . Do not be overcome by evil, but overcome evil with good.

Romans 12:17, 19, 21 NIV

Prayer

Lord, I am ashamed at how often I am tempted to be dishonest. The little white lies, the half truths, fall so smoothly off my tongue. All too many times your still small voice inside has let me know how completely you see through me. Thank you for not giving up on me. I ask your forgiveness for the lame excuses I have offered to you for my lack of honesty in word and deed. God of all truth, help me to break the patterns of dishonesty that hinder my relationship with you and in so doing to reflect your truth to the world.

Promise

Look at those who are honest and good, for a wonderful future lies before those who love peace.

Psalm 37:37 NLT

ILLNESS

*The hedge (illness) can cut off the world and confine on
every side, but it cannot shut out our view of the skies nor
prevent the soul from looking up into the face of God. Indeed, because there is so little else he can see, and because
he needs God so badly, the hedged-in Christian, if he will,
may possibly learn to see God more clearly and to know
Him more truly than his brother who seems to be free to
live life more fully.*

—Margaret Clarkson, *Grace Grows Best in Winter*

**1. Suffering can be used by the Lord to renew us in-
wardly and to achieve an eternal glory that outweighs all
of our suffering.**

That is why we never give up. Though our bodies are dying,
our spirits are being renewed every day. For our present troubles are quite small and won't last very long. Yet they produce
for us an immeasurably great glory that will last forever! So we
don't look at the troubles we can see right now; rather, we look

93

forward to what we have not yet seen. For the troubles we see will soon be over, but the joys to come will last forever.

2 Corinthians 4:16–18 NLT

✦ He gives strength to the weary, and to him who lacks might He increases power. Though youths grow weary and tired, and vigorous young men stumble badly, yet those who wait for the LORD will gain new strength; they will mount up with wings like eagles, they will run and not get tired, they will walk and not become weary.

Isaiah 40:29–31 NASB

2. During Christ's earthly ministry, he showed compassion for people by healing them from their illnesses.

✦ Jesus went throughout Galilee, teaching in their synagogues, preaching the good news of the kingdom, and healing every disease and sickness among the people.

Matthew 4:23 NIV

✦ But Simon's wife's mother lay sick with a fever, and they told Him about her at once. So He came and took her by the hand and lifted her up, and immediately the fever left her. And she served them. Now at evening, when the sun had set, they brought to Him all who were sick and those who were demon-possessed. And the whole city was gathered together at the door. Then He healed many who were sick with various diseases, and cast out many demons.

Mark 1:30–34 NKJV

✦ And Jesus said to him, "Receive your sight; your faith has made you well." Immediately he regained his sight and began following Him, glorifying God; and when all the people saw it, they gave praise to God.

Luke 18:42–43 NASB

3. Times of illness remind us of our dependence on the Lord.

I think you ought to know, dear friends, about the trouble we went through in the province of Asia. We were crushed and completely overwhelmed, and we thought we would never live through it. In fact, we expected to die. But as a result, we learned not to rely on ourselves, but on God who can raise the dead. And he did deliver us from mortal danger. And we are confident that he will continue to deliver us.

2 Corinthians 1:8–10 NLT

4. Sometimes an illness is the result of deliberate acts of sin.

When I kept silent, my bones wasted away through my groaning all day long. For day and night your hand was heavy upon me; my strength was sapped as in the heat of summer. Then I acknowledged my sin to you and did not cover up my iniquity.

Psalm 32:3–5 NIV

A raging fever burns within me, and my health is broken. I am exhausted and completely crushed. My groans come from an anguished heart. . . . My heart beats wildly, my strength fails, and I am going blind.

Psalm 38:7, 8, 10 NLT

"O LORD," I prayed, "have mercy on me. Heal me, for I have sinned against you."

Psalm 41:4 NLT

Therefore, whoever eats the bread or drinks the cup of the Lord in an unworthy manner will be guilty of sinning against the body and blood of the Lord. A man ought to examine himself before he eats of the bread and drinks of the cup. For anyone who eats and drinks without recognizing the body of the Lord eats and drinks judgment on himself. That is why many among you are weak and sick, and a number of you have fallen asleep.

1 Corinthians 11:27–30 NIV

5. We should not conclude that all illnesses in our lives are the direct results of particular sins. Nor are we to conclude that illnesses in others are the result of specific sins they have committed.

↠ And His disciples asked Him, saying, "Rabbi, who sinned, this man or his parents, that he was born blind?" Jesus answered, "Neither this man nor his parents sinned, but that the works of God should be revealed in him."

John 9:2–3 NKJV

↠ Or those eighteen on whom the tower in Siloam fell and killed them, do you think that they were worse sinners than all other men who dwelt in Jerusalem? I tell you, no.

Luke 13:3–4 NKJV

6. We have the opportunity as members of Christ's church to request that our elders pray for us and anoint us with oil when we are ill.

↠ Are any among you sick? They should call for the elders of the church and have them pray over them, anointing them with oil in the name of the Lord. And their prayer offered in faith will heal the sick, and the Lord will make them well. And anyone who has committed sins will be forgiven.

James 5:14–15 NLT

7. A cheerful spirit and peaceful life can foster good health.

↠ A heart at peace gives life to the body, but envy rots the bones.

Proverbs 14:30 NIV

↠ A cheerful look brings joy to the heart, and good news gives health to the bones.

Proverbs 15:30 NIV

⁊⁊ Pleasant words are a honeycomb, sweet to the soul and healing to the bones.

Proverbs 16:24 NIV

⁊⁊ A cheerful heart is good medicine, but a crushed spirit dries up the bones.

Proverbs 17:22 NIV

8. The Bible's words of life are important for sustaining and restoring health to our bodies.

⁊⁊ My son, pay attention to what I say; listen closely to my words. Do not let them out of your sight, keep them within your heart; for they are life to those who find them and health to a man's whole body.

Proverbs 4:20–22 NIV

9. God is able to grant sufficient grace for his people to endure in situations where he does not immediately remove their illnesses.

⁊⁊ And lest I should be exalted above measure by the abundance of the revelations, a thorn in the flesh was given to me, a messenger of Satan to buffet me, lest I be exalted above measure. Concerning this thing I pleaded with the Lord three times that it might depart from me. And He said to me, "My grace is sufficient for you, for My strength is made perfect in weakness." Therefore most gladly I will rather boast in my infirmities, that the power of Christ may rest upon me. Therefore I take pleasure in infirmities, in reproaches, in needs, in persecutions, in distresses, for Christ's sake. For when I am weak, then I am strong.

2 Corinthians 12:7–10 NKJV

⁊⁊ The LORD nurses them when they are sick and eases their pain and discomfort.

Psalm 41:3 NLT

10. Receiving God's comfort in times of illness and suffering prepares us to offer that same comfort to others.

~ Praise be to the God and Father of our Lord Jesus Christ, the Father of compassion and the God of all comfort, who comforts us in all our troubles, so that we can comfort those in any trouble with the comfort we ourselves have received from God.

2 Corinthians 1:3–4 NIV

11. God deserves our praise when he chooses to bless us by healing our diseases.

~ Bless the LORD, O my soul, and all that is within me, bless His holy name. Bless the LORD, O my soul, and forget none of His benefits; who pardons all your iniquities, who heals all your diseases.

Psalm 103:1–3 NASB

12. The unending joy of heaven will not be interrupted by illness or suffering of any kind.

~ He will wipe away every tear from their eyes; and there will no longer be any death; there will no longer be any mourning, or crying, or pain; the first things have passed away.

Revelation 21:4 NASB

Prayer

Lord, you've got my attention. If pain is your megaphone, I'm all ears. I don't pretend to enjoy the prospects of an extended illness. The thought of coping with pain and immobility for who knows how long frightens me. If it is your will, please deliver me from this suffering and from the feelings of fear and helplessness that accompany it.

Remind me on those occasions when I hit rock bottom that I never suffer alone. I ask for the strength to choose to love you—even when that choice involves pain. My earnest prayer is that you will use my suffering as a preparation for future ministry.

Promise

He gives strength to the weary, and to him who lacks might He increases power. Though youths grow weary and tired, and vigorous young men stumble badly, yet those who wait for the LORD will gain new strength; they will mount up with wings like eagles, they will run and not get tired, they will walk and not become weary.

Isaiah 40:29–31 NASB

INCENTIVES FOR PRAYER

The prayer life of the Christian is the true gauge of the rest of his life. No one's outer life of activity ever rises above one's inner life of prayer. As you pray, so are you. You never become a better Christian than you are in your prayer life. No matter how zealous, how busy, how benevolent, how good a name you may have as a Christian worker, teacher or preacher, you are no better than when you are alone with God in prayer. What you are and do in secret will appear openly. If you are weak, lacking and powerless there, you will be weak and lacking in spiritual power at every other point in your Christian character and activities. Everything as to what you become and as to what you accomplish for the Glory of God and His Kingdom depends upon prayer as it depends on nothing else in the world.

—Author Unknown

1. We are urged in Scripture to be faithful in prayer throughout our lifetime.

Pray without ceasing.

1 Thessalonians 5:17

I urge that entreaties and prayers, petitions and thanksgivings, be made on behalf of all men, for kings and all who are in authority, so that we may lead a tranquil and quiet life in all godliness and dignity. This is good and acceptable in the sight of God our Savior.

1 Timothy 2:1–3 NASB

So wherever you assemble, I want men to pray with holy hands lifted up to God, free from anger and controversy.

1 Timothy 2:8 NLT

2. Christ, who is our example, modeled a vital prayer life.

He went out into a mountain to pray, and continued all night in prayer to God.

Luke 6:12

He withdrew from them about a stone's throw, and He knelt down and began to pray.

Luke 22:41 NASB

And being in an agony he prayed more earnestly: and his sweat was as it were great drops of blood falling down to the ground.

Luke 22:44

3. Knowing that Christ, who is our high priest, is able to sympathize with our human weaknesses motivates us to pray.

For we do not have a high priest who is unable to sympathize with our weaknesses, but we have one who has been tempted in every way, just as we are—yet was without sin. Let us then approach the throne of grace with confidence, so that we may receive mercy and find grace to help us in our time of need.

Hebrews 4:15–16 NIV

101

⟊ Casting all your care upon him; for he careth for you.

1 Peter 5:7

4. The certainty that God hears our prayers enables us to pray with confidence.

⟊ But when you pray, go away by yourself, shut the door behind you, and pray to your Father secretly. Then your Father, who knows all secrets, will reward you.

Matthew 6:6 NLT

⟊ I cried unto the LORD with my voice, and he heard me out of his holy hill.

Psalm 3:4

⟊ In the morning, O LORD, you hear my voice; in the morning I lay my requests before you and wait in expectation.

Psalm 5:3 NIV

5. Scripture repeatedly assures us that the prayers of God's people are effective.

⟊ The effective prayer of a righteous man can accomplish much. Elijah was a man with a nature like ours, and he prayed earnestly that it would not rain, and it did not rain on the earth for three years and six months. Then he prayed again, and the sky poured rain and the earth produced its fruit.

James 5:16b–18 NASB

⟊ This is the confidence we have in approaching God: that if we ask anything according to his will, he hears us. And if we know that he hears us—whatever we ask—we know that we have what we asked of him.

1 John 5:14–15 NIV

⟊ If you abide in Me, and My words abide in you, you will ask what you desire, and it shall be done for you.

John 15:7 NKJV

⁓ If I regard iniquity in my heart, the Lord will not hear. But certainly God has heard me; He has attended to the voice of my prayer. Blessed be God, Who has not turned away my prayer, nor His mercy from me!

Psalm 66:18–20 NKJV

⁓ The Lord is far from the wicked: but he heareth the prayer of the righteous.

Proverbs 15:29

6. The Book of Revelation teaches that the prayers of believing saints reach the throne of God in heaven.

⁓ And as he took the scroll, the four living beings and the twenty-four elders fell down before the Lamb. Each one had a harp, and they held gold bowls filled with incense—the prayers of God's people!

Revelation 5:8 NLT

7. Prayer is an antidote to worry and discouragement.

⁓ Then He spoke a parable to them, that men always ought to pray and not lose heart.

Luke 18:1 NKJV

⁓ Be anxious for nothing, but in everything by prayer and supplication, with thanksgiving, let your requests be made known to God; and the peace of God, which surpasses all understanding, will guard your hearts and minds through Christ Jesus.

Philippians 4:6–7 NKJV

8. The Lord sometimes blesses us with answers to our prayers beyond our wildest expectations.

⁓ Call to Me and I will answer you, and I will tell you great and mighty things, which you do not know.

Jeremiah 33:3 NASB

↜ Now glory be to God! By his mighty power at work within us, he is able to accomplish infinitely more than we would ever dare to ask or hope.

Ephesians 3:20 NLT

Prayer

Father, I bow before you, to praise and thank you for opening a way of access to your throne through Christ my Savior. I am humbled that you desire my prayers at all. I acknowledge that my spiritual effectiveness depends upon prayer as it depends upon nothing else in this world. Yet I confess that too often I become distracted and apathetic. Too often I pray only when facing urgent needs. Forgive me, Lord. Help me to develop a disciplined and vital prayer life. Remind me of the incentives to prayer that you have given in Scripture. I believe that you are able by your mighty power at work in me to accomplish far more than what I would ever dare to ask or hope. Thank you for hearing me now as I pray in Jesus' name.

Promise

This is the confidence we have in approaching God: that if we ask anything according to his will, he hears us. And if we know that he hears us—whatever we ask—we know that we have what we asked of him.

1 John 5:14–15 NIV

INTERPERSONAL CONFLICTS

How effective the church would be in our day if it could become a great healer in the legal arena—a great restorer of relationships, peace, and harmony. Imagine the powerful witness of reconciled Jews and gentiles in the first century. Here were hostile people, who had been separated and alienated, now praying, rejoicing, and ministering together. Perhaps the declaration of Christ's reconciliation was easier to believe because the world saw it manifested in the believing community's relationships.

—Lynn R. Buzzard and Laurence Eck, *Tell It to the Church*

1. Scripture realistically assumes that life in a fallen world involves interpersonal conflict.

✦ Where do wars and fights come from among you?

James 4:1 NKJV

✦ If you keep on biting and devouring each other, watch out or you will be destroyed by each other.

Galatians 5:15 NIV

r . . . disputes, dissentions, factions.

Galatians 5:20 NASB

r Endeavoring to keep the unity of the Spirit in the bond of peace.

Ephesians 4:3 NKJV

2. Avoidable conflicts often erupt when people give vent to selfish desires and fail to respect the interests of others.

r What is causing the quarrels and fights among you? Isn't it the whole army of evil desires at war within you? You want what you don't have, so you scheme and kill to get it. You are jealous for what others have, and you can't possess it, so you fight and quarrel to take it away from them. And yet the reason you don't have what you want is that you don't ask God for it. And even when you do ask, you don't get it because your whole motive is wrong—you want only what will give you pleasure.

James 4:1–3 NLT

r Do nothing from selfishness or empty conceit, but with humility of mind regard one another as more important than yourselves; do not merely look out for your own personal interests, but also for the interests of others.

Philippians 2:3–4 NASB

3. Scripture warns us that the expression of uncontrolled anger destroys human relationships.

r A fool always loses his temper, but a wise man holds it back.

Proverbs 29:11 NASB

r For as churning the milk produces butter, and as twisting the nose produces blood, so stirring up anger produces strife.

Proverbs 30:33 NIV

⁓ A gentle answer turns away wrath, but a harsh word stirs up anger.

Proverbs 15:1 NIV

⁓ And "don't sin by letting anger gain control over you." Don't let the sun go down while you are still angry, for anger gives a mighty foothold to the Devil.

Ephesians 4:26–27 NLT

⁓ For the anger of man does not achieve the righteousness of God.

James 1:20 NASB

4. Interpersonal conflict can arise between a believer and a nonbeliever because of the believer's allegiance to Christ. Those who are insulted because of the name of Christ are promised a future reward.

⁓ But even if you suffer for doing what is right, God will reward you for it. . . . Keep your conscience clear. Then if people speak evil against you, they will be ashamed when they see what a good life you live because you belong to Christ.

1 Peter 3:14, 16 NLT

⁓ Be happy if you are insulted for being a Christian, for then the glorious Spirit of God will come upon you. If you suffer, however, it must not be for murder, stealing, making trouble, or prying into other people's affairs. But it is no shame to suffer for being a Christian. Praise God for the privilege of being called by his wonderful name!

1 Peter 4:14–16 NLT

5. We must not allow bitterness to poison our relationships. Instead we should cultivate a spirit of compassion and exhibit a readiness to forgive.

↝ For if you forgive men their trespasses, your heavenly Father will also forgive you. But if you do not forgive men their trespasses, neither will your Father forgive your trespasses.

Matthew 6:14–15 NKJV

↝ Get rid of all bitterness, rage, anger, harsh words, and slander, as well as all types of malicious behavior. Instead, be kind to each other, tenderhearted, forgiving one another, just as God through Christ has forgiven you.

Ephesians 4:31–32 NLT

↝ So, as those who have been chosen by God, holy and beloved, put on a heart of compassion, kindness, humility, gentleness and patience; bearing with one another, and forgiving each other, whoever has a complaint against anyone; just as the Lord forgave you, so also should you.

Colossians 3:12–13 NASB

↝ Therefore, rid yourselves of all malice and all deceit, hypocrisy, envy, and slander of every kind.

1 Peter 2:1 NIV

6. Interpersonal conflict can be diminished or sometimes avoided if we follow the scriptural injunction to use speech constructively rather than destructively.

↝ Do not let any unwholesome talk come out of your mouths, but only what is helpful for building others up according to their needs, that it may benefit those who listen.

Ephesians 4:29 NIV

7. A believer's willingness to forego revenge can be used by God to overcome evil with good.

↝ Never pay back evil for evil to anyone. Respect what is right in the sight of all men. If possible, so far as it depends on you, be at peace with all men. Never take your own revenge, beloved, but leave room for the wrath of God, for it is written, "Vengeance is Mine, I will repay," says the Lord. "But if your enemy is hungry, feed him, and if he is thirsty, give him a drink; for in so doing you will heap burning coals on his head." Do not be overcome by evil, but overcome evil with good.

Romans 12:17–21 NASB

8. If conflict develops to the point that someone becomes our enemy, we should pray for them faithfully and minister lovingly to their physical needs.

⏺ If your enemy is hungry, give him bread to eat; and if he is thirsty, give him water to drink; for so you will heap coals of fire on his head, and the Lord will reward you.

Proverbs 25:21–22 NKJV

⏺ But I say, love your enemies! Pray for those who persecute you! In that way, you will be acting as true children of your Father in heaven. For he gives his sunlight to both the evil and the good, and he sends rain on the just and on the unjust, too. If you love only those who love you, what good is that? Even corrupt tax collectors do that much.

Matthew 5:44–46 NLT

9. Christians should have a reputation for being the ones who initiate conflict resolution.

⏺ Blessed are the peacemakers, for they shall be called sons of God.

Matthew 5:9 NKJV

⏺ If it is possible, as much as depends on you, live peaceably with all men.

Romans 12:18 NKJV

⏺ Let us therefore make every effort to do what leads to peace and to mutual edification.

Romans 14:19 NIV

109

↝ Let the peace of Christ rule in your hearts, since as members of one body you were called to peace.

Colossians 3:15 NIV

↝ Let us not become weary in doing good, for at the proper time we will reap a harvest if we do not give up. Therefore, as we have opportunity, let us do good to all people, especially to those who belong to the family of believers.

Galatians 6:9–10 NIV

10. When significant ruptures develop between two Christians, each party is responsible to take the initiative to go to the other person in an effort to resolve the conflict.

↝ Therefore if you are presenting your offering at the altar, and there remember that your brother has something against you, leave your offering there before the altar and go; first be reconciled to your brother, and then come and present your offering.

Matthew 5:23–24 NASB

↝ If your brother sins, go and show him his fault in private; if he listens to you, you have won your brother. But if he does not listen to you, take one or two more with you, so that by the mouth of two or three witnesses every fact may be confirmed. If he refuses to listen to them, tell it to the church; and if he refuses to listen even to the church, let him be to you as a Gentile and a tax collector.

Matthew 18:15–17 NASB

11. The example of a difference of opinion between Paul and Barnabas illustrates how sometimes we simply need to agree to disagree with a Christian brother or sister.

↝ Barnabas wanted to take John, also called Mark, with them, but Paul did not think it wise to take him, because he had deserted them in Pamphylia and had not continued with them in the work. They had such a sharp disagreement that they parted company. Barnabas took Mark and sailed for Cyprus, but Paul chose Silas and left, commended by the brothers to the grace of the Lord.

Acts 15:37–40 NIV

Prayer

Father, you have designed that your children live in fellowship with one another. As I reflect on these Scriptures, I am troubled and saddened because a relationship I value has gone sour through a series of misunderstandings. I ask your forgiveness for the extent to which I am at fault. Help me to handle my feelings of resentment and mistreatment in a biblical manner and be willing to take the initiative to restore harmony in this fractured relationship. I especially need your guidance because up to this point, my feeble attempts at restoration have seemed to make the situation worse. Give me the mind of Christ, the unselfish mind of a servant, as I pursue a biblical solution. I ask that by your grace and power, this wound may yet be healed.

Promise

Blessed are the peacemakers, for they shall be called sons of God.

Matthew 5:9 NKJV

111

LEARNING PATIENCE

Patience is the result of well-centered strength. To "wait on the Lord," to "rest in the Lord," is an indication of a healthy, holy faith, while impatience is an indication of an unhealthy, unholy unbelief.

—Oswald Chambers, *Spiritual Disciplines*

1. Our Lord is patient in his dealings with us and even with those who resist him.

And the LORD passed by before him, and proclaimed, the LORD, the LORD God, merciful and gracious, longsuffering, and abundant in goodness and truth.

Exodus 34:6

But You, O Lord, are a God full of compassion, and gracious, longsuffering and abundant in mercy and truth.

Psalm 86:15 NKJV

❧ Don't you realize how kind, tolerant, and patient God is with you? Or don't you care? Can't you see how kind he has been in giving you time to turn from your sin?

Romans 2:4 NLT

❧ God has every right to exercise his judgment and his power, but he also has the right to be very patient with those who are the objects of his judgment and are fit only for destruction.

Romans 9:22 NLT

❧ God waited patiently in the days of Noah while the ark was being built.

1 Peter 3:20 NIV

❧ The Lord is not slow in keeping his promise, as some understand slowness. He is patient with you, not wanting anyone to perish, but everyone to come to repentance. . . . Bear in mind that our Lord's patience means salvation.

2 Peter 3:9, 15 NIV

2. Scripture repeatedly encourages us to demonstrate patience in our relationships with others.

❧ Love is patient and kind.

1 Corinthians 13:4 NLT

❧ Therefore I, the prisoner of the Lord, implore you to walk in a manner worthy of the calling with which you have been called, with all humility and gentleness, with patience, showing tolerance for one another in love.

Ephesians 4:1–2 NASB

❧ Therefore, as God's chosen people, holy and dearly loved, clothe yourselves with compassion, kindness, humility, gentleness, and patience. Bear with each other and forgive whatever grievances you may have against one another.

Colossians 3:12–13 NIV

113

↝ And we urge you, brothers, warn those who are idle, encourage the timid, help the weak, be patient with everyone.

1 Thessalonians 5:14 NIV

↝ Patiently correct, rebuke, and encourage your people with good teaching.

2 Timothy 4:2 NLT

3. Patience and longsuffering in the face of testing builds spiritual maturity.

↝ Patient in tribulation.

Romans 12:12

↝ We also glory in tribulations, knowing that tribulation produces perseverance; and perseverance, character; and character, hope.

Romans 5:3–4 NKJV

↝ We proudly tell God's other churches about your endurance and faithfulness in all the persecutions and hardships you are suffering. But God will use this persecution to show his justice. For he will make you worthy of his Kingdom, for which you are suffering.

2 Thessalonians 1:4–5 NLT

↝ Knowing that the testing of your faith produces patience. But let patience have its perfect work, that you may be perfect and complete, lacking nothing.

James 1:3–4 NKJV

↝ Make every effort to add to your faith goodness; and to goodness, knowledge; and to knowledge, self-control; and to self-control, perseverance; and to perseverance, godliness.

2 Peter 1:5–6 NIV

4. Scripture encourages us with examples of patience in the lives of believers who have gone before us.

114

↝ And so, having patiently waited, he [Abraham] obtained the promise.

Hebrews 6:15 NASB

↝ Therefore, since we are surrounded by such a great cloud of witnesses, let us throw off everything that hinders and the sin that so easily entangles, and let us run with perseverance the race marked out for us.

Hebrews 12:1 NIV

↝ As an example, brethren, of suffering and patience, take the prophets who spoke in the name of the Lord. We count those blessed who endured. You have heard of the endurance of Job and have seen the outcome of the Lord's dealings, that the Lord is full of compassion and is merciful.

James 5:10–11 NASB

↝ Such things were written in the Scriptures long ago to teach us. They give us hope and encouragement as we wait patiently for God's promises. May God, who gives this patience and encouragement, help you live in complete harmony with each other—each with the attitude of Christ Jesus toward the other.

Romans 15:4–5 NLT

5. Scripture instructs us to wait patiently for the promised return of Christ.

↝ Dear brothers and sisters, you must be patient as you wait for the Lord's return. Consider the farmers who eagerly look for the rains in the fall and in the spring. They patiently wait for the precious harvest to ripen. You, too, must be patient. And take courage, for the coming of the Lord is near.

James 5:7–8 NLT

6. Patience is produced in us by God's Spirit as we wait upon him.

115

↜ But the fruit of the Spirit is . . . patience.

Galatians 5:22 NIV

↜ Rest in the LORD and wait patiently for Him.

Psalm 37:7 NASB

↜ I waited patiently for the LORD; and He inclined to me and heard my cry.

Psalm 40:1 NASB

↜ Those who wait on the LORD will find new strength. They will fly high on wings like eagles. They will run and not grow weary. They will walk and not faint.

Isaiah 40:31 NLT

Prayer

Lord, thank you for your patience with me over the years. I confess I have a long way to go before this fruit of the Spirit is ripened in my life. Too often I do not respond with patience to the big and little irritants that cross my path. On the job, in the home, behind the steering wheel, my patience is lost all too easily. I have even dared to grow impatient with your plan and purposes for my life. Please forgive my audacity. I desire to be a living object lesson of patience in all my conduct and relationships.

Promise

Dear brothers and sisters, you must be patient as you wait for the Lord's return. Consider the farmers who eagerly look for the rains in the fall and in the spring. They patiently wait for the precious harvest to ripen. You, too, must be patient. And take courage, for the coming of the Lord is near.

James 5:7–8 NLT

116

LONELINESS

The knowledge that we are never alone calms the troubled sea of our lives and speaks peace to our souls.

—A. W. Tozer, *The Knowledge of the Holy*

1. The assurance of God's constant presence comforts us in times of loneliness.

You know when I sit and when I rise; you perceive my thoughts from afar. You discern my going out and my lying down; you are familiar with all my ways. . . . Where can I go from your Spirit? Where can I flee from your presence?

Psalm 139: 2–3, 7 NIV

2. God has designed that the church as a unified body ministers to the needs of each of its members, including the need for encouraging companionship.

And let us consider one another in order to stir up love and good works, not forsaking the assembling of ourselves together,

117

as is the manner of some, but exhorting one another, and so much the more as you see the Day approaching.

Hebrews 10:24–25 NKJV

↝ But in fact God has arranged the parts in the body, every one of them, just as he wanted them to be. If they were all one part, where would the body be? As it is, there are many parts, but one body. . . . If one part suffers, every part suffers with it; if one part is honored, every part rejoices with it.

1 Corinthians 12:18–20, 26 NIV

3. At the beginning of history God recognized our innate need for companionship by creating marriage as one way to combat loneliness.

↝ And the LORD God said, "It is not good that man should be alone; I will make him a helper comparable to him."

Genesis 2:18 NKJV

↝ The wife of your youth . . . she is your companion.

Malachi 2:14 NKJV

↝ The man who finds a wife finds a treasure and receives favor from the LORD.

Proverbs 18:22 NLT

4. God recognizes the value of family relationships as one of the answers to loneliness.

↝ God places the lonely in families.

Psalm 68:6 NLT

5. God provides friendships as a means of meeting our needs.

↞ A man who has friends must himself be friendly, but there is a friend who sticks closer than a brother.

Proverbs 18:24 NKJV

↞ If one persons falls, the other can reach out and help. But people who are alone when they fall are in real trouble. And on a cold night, two under the same blanket can gain warmth from each other. But how can one be warm alone? A person standing alone can be attacked and defeated, but two can stand back-to-back and conquer. Three are even better, for a triple-braided cord is not easily broken.

Ecclesiastes 4:10–12 NLT

6. Christ modeled for us the importance of taking time to be alone with God.

↞ After He had sent the crowds away, He went up on the mountain by Himself to pray; and when it was evening, He was there alone.

Matthew 14:23 NASB

↞ In the early morning, while it was still dark, Jesus got up, left the house, and went away to a secluded place, and was praying there.

Mark 1:35 NASB

↞ And it happened that while He was praying alone, the disciples were with Him, and He questioned them, saying "Who do the people say that I am?"

Luke 9:18 NASB

↞ Jesus saw that they were ready to take him by force and make him king, so he went higher into the hills alone.

John 6:15 NLT

119

~ A time is coming, and has come, when you will be scattered, each to his own home. You will leave me all alone. Yet I am not alone, for my Father is with me.

John 16:32 NIV

7. In times of loneliness it is helpful to recall and give thanks for Christ's promise that he will never ever abandon us.

~ Be strong and courageous! Do not be afraid of them! The LORD your God will go ahead of you. He will neither fail you nor forsake you.

Deuteronomy 31:6 NLT

~ I am with you always, even to the end of the age.

Matthew 28:20 NKJV

~ Keep your lives free from the love of money and be content with what you have, because God has said, "Never will I leave you; never will I forsake you."

Hebrews 13:5 NIV

~ The Lord is near.

Philippians 4:4 NIV

Prayer

I'm lonely, Lord. There seems to be no one with whom I can share my deepest feelings. It comforts me to know that my trials and my tears do not go unnoticed by you.

Thank you for sending your Son into this broken world full of lonely people like me. I am reminded of the unspeakable anguish of Gethsemane that your Son endured alone while his disciples slept. My loneliness pales in comparison.

Thank you for your promise never to leave me or forsake me. Help me to live each moment in the assurance of your love and with the knowledge that I am never truly alone.

Promise

Be strong and courageous! Do not be afraid of them! The LORD your God will go ahead of you. He will neither fail you nor forsake you.

Deuteronomy 31:6 NLT

MARITAL CONFLICT

Living for the one who loved us when we were yet his enemies teaches us what it means for each to live for the other in marriage when no other earthly cause may justify our continuing union. The Lord who died for us teaches us that when we give of ourselves for another—dying to ourselves in the process—we discover what it really means to live, and enjoy most fully what it really means to love. Our Lord makes our lives as sweet as heaven desires by drawing our hearts together in love for him.

—Bryan Chapell, *Each for the Other*

1. A healthy relationship between husbands and wives is vital. It reflects to the world the relationship between Christ and his bride, the church.

↞ And you husbands must love your wives with the same love Christ shows the church. He gave up his life for her to make her holy and clean, washed by baptism and God's word. He did this to present her to himself as a glorious church without a spot or wrinkle or any other blemish. Instead, she will be holy and without fault.

Ephesians 5:25–27 NLT

2. In marriage, each partner's relationship with God is strongly influenced by the relationship with one's mate.

⤚ Husbands, in the same way be considerate as you live with your wives, and treat them with respect as the weaker partner and as heirs with you of the gracious gift of life, so that nothing will hinder your prayers.

1 Peter 3:7 NIV

3. The resolution of conflicts in marriage should begin with honest self-examination rather than focusing on the problems in one's mate.

⤚ Why do you look at the speck of sawdust in your brother's eye and pay no attention to the plank in your own eye? How can you say to your brother, "Let me take the speck out of your eye," when all the time there is a plank in your own eye? You hypocrite, first take the plank out of your own eye, and then you will see clearly to remove the speck from your brother's eye.

Matthew 7:3–5 NIV

4. A self-centered outlook on life is often the root of an unhealthy marriage relationship.

⤚ Do nothing from selfishness or empty conceit, but with humility of mind regard one another as more important than yourselves; do not merely look out for your own personal interests, but also for the interests of others.

Philippians 2:3–4 NASB

123

5. Marital problems can develop when couples fail to recognize that marriage is designed by God to be a covenant of companionship.

↞ The LORD God said, "It is not good for the man to be alone. I will make a helper suitable for him."

Genesis 2:18 NIV

↞ She is your companion and your wife by covenant.

Malachi 2:14 NKJV

6. Marital conflicts quickly surface when marriage is viewed as a convenient arrangement to meet one's own preconceived needs rather than an unselfish giving of oneself to meet a partner's needs.

↞ For God so loved the world that He gave . . .

John 3:16 NKJV

↞ Husbands, love your wives, just as Christ also loved the church and gave Himself for it.

Ephesians 5:25 NKJV

7. Unnecessary strain is placed on marriage partners when God's plan for self-giving sexual relationships is ignored.

↞ The husband should fulfill his marital duty to his wife, and likewise the wife to her husband. The wife's body does not belong to her alone but also to her husband. In the same way, the husband's body does not belong to him alone but also to his wife. Do not deprive each other except by mutual consent and for a time, so that you may devote yourselves to prayer. Then come together again so that Satan will not tempt you because of your lack of self-control.

1 Corinthians 7:3–5 NIV

8. Tensions between marriage partners are exacerbated by harsh language.

✏ Don't use foul or abusive language. Let everything you say be good and helpful, so that your words will be an encouragement to those who hear them. . . . Get rid of all bitterness, rage, anger, harsh words, and slander, as well as all types of malicious behavior. Instead, be kind to each other, tenderhearted, forgiving one another, just as God through Christ has forgiven you.

Ephesians 4:29, 31–32 NLT

9. Marital tensions that center around money may be due to an idolatrous love of money and an accompanying failure to learn contentment.

✏ But godliness actually is a means of great gain when accompanied by contentment. For we have brought nothing into the world, so we cannot take anything out of it either. If we have food and covering, with these we shall be content. But those who want to get rich fall into temptation and a snare and many foolish and harmful desires which plunge men into ruin and destruction. For the love of money is a root of all sorts of evil, and some by longing for it have wandered away from the faith and pierced themselves with many griefs.

1 Timothy 6:6–10 NASB

10. Some marital problems are caused by a foolish misuse of alcohol.

✏ And do not be drunk with wine, in which is dissipation; but be filled with the Spirit.

Ephesians 5:18 NKJV

✏ Wine is a mocker and beer a brawler; whoever is led astray by them is not wise.

Proverbs 20:1 NIV

125

✦ Do not mix with winebibbers.

Proverbs 23:20 NKJV

✦ Who has woe? Who has sorrow? Who has contentions? Who has complaints? Who has wounds without cause? Who has redness of eyes? Those who linger long at the wine, those who go in search of mixed wine.

Proverbs 23:29–30 NKJV

11. Unnecessary marital conflict can arise when anger is allowed to spill over from one day to the next.

✦ And "don't sin by letting anger gain control over you." Don't let the sun go down while you are still angry, for anger gives a mighty foothold to the Devil.

Ephesians 4:26–27 NLT

12. Marital problems should be faced with a willingness to make allowances for the weaknesses of one's mate and a willingness to offer forgiveness.

✦ Bear with each other and forgive whatever grievances you may have against one another. Forgive as the Lord forgave you.

Colossians 3:13 NIV

13. Conflicts within marriage should be approached with a conscious desire to implement the quality of love described in Scripture.

✦ Love is patient, love is kind. It does not envy, it does not boast, it is not proud. It is not rude, it is not self-seeking, it is not easily angered, it keeps no record of wrongs. Love does not delight in evil but rejoices with the truth. It always protects, always trusts, always hopes, always perseveres.

1 Corinthians 13:4–7 NIV

14. God's enabling resources and his promised presence and comfort can equip believers in times of marital conflict and even marriage breakup.

∼ God is our refuge and strength, a very present help in trouble. Therefore we will not fear, though the earth should change and though the mountains slip into the heart of the sea.

Psalm 46:1–2 NASB

∼ The LORD says, "I will rescue those who love me. I will protect those who trust in my name. When they call on me, I will answer, I will be with them in trouble. I will rescue them and honor them."

Psalm 91:14–15 NLT

Prayer

Lord, we were supposed to cherish and support each other, but that is not the way things really are in our marriage. The familiar words "happily ever after" and "till death do us part" have a hollow ring as I struggle with feelings of bitterness and disillusionment. I ask for your forgiveness for the extent to which I am at fault for the conflicts and failures in my marriage.

Thank you that you are a God of restoration. From this moment on, I desire that my life be characterized by an attitude of self-sacrificing humility and love and a willingness to offer and receive forgiveness. Please replace my fear of tomorrow with confidence in your adequacy to meet my needs and the needs of my mate. I commit my uncertain future to you and ask for the faith to trust in your sovereignty, not as a trite cliché, but as my center of gravity.

127

Promise

You will keep him in perfect peace, whose mind is stayed on You, because he trusts in You.

Isaiah 26:3 NKJV

MORAL PURITY

God expects us to assume our responsibilities for keeping the sinful desires of the body under control. It is true we cannot do this in our own strength. Our sinful desires, stimulated by all the temptations around us, are too strong for us. But though we cannot do it by ourselves, we can do it. As we set ourselves to the task in dependence upon the Holy Spirit, we will see Him at work in us.

—Jerry Bridges, *The Pursuit of Holiness*

1. Moral purity is rooted in the holiness of God.

Your eyes are too pure to approve evil, and You cannot look on wickedness with favor.

Habakkuk 1:13 NASB

This High Priest of ours understands our weaknesses, for he faced all of the same temptations we do, yet he did not sin.

Hebrews 4:15 NLT

He is the kind of high priest we need because he is holy and blameless, unstained by sin. He has now been set apart from sinners, and he has been given the highest place of honor in heaven. He does not need to offer sacrifices every day like the other high priests. They did this for their own sins first and then for the sins of the people. But Jesus did this once for all when he sacrificed himself on the cross.

Hebrews 7:26–27 NLT

↝ Be ye holy; for I am holy.

1 Peter 1:16

2. To see God and worship in his presence requires moral purity.

↝ Who may ascend the hill of the LORD? Who may stand in his holy place? He who has clean hands and a pure heart, who does not lift up his soul to an idol or swear by what is false.

Psalm 24:3–4 NIV

↝ Blessed are the pure in heart: for they shall see God.

Matthew 5:8

↝ Flee also youthful lusts: but follow righteousness, faith, charity, peace, with them that call on the Lord out of a pure heart.

2 Timothy 2:22

↝ Pursue peace with all men, and holiness, without which no one will see the Lord.

Hebrews 12:14 NKJV

3. The Lord expects that we resist and flee from immoral behavior.

↝ Abstain . . . from sexuality immorality.

Acts 15:20 NKJV

↝ You shall not commit adultery.

Exodus 20:14 NKJV

↤ Flee from sexual immorality. All other sins a man commits are outside his body, but he who sins sexually sins against his own body. Do you not know that your body is a temple of the Holy Spirit, who is in you, whom you have received from God? You are not your own.

1 Corinthians 6:18–19 NIV

↤ God wants you to be holy, so you should keep clear of all sexual sin. Then each of you will control your body and live in holiness and honor—not in lustful passion as the pagans do, in their ignorance of God and his ways.

1 Thessalonians 4:3–5 NLT

↤ Flee also youthful lusts: but follow righteousness, faith, charity, peace, with them that call on the Lord out of a pure heart.

2 Timothy 2:22

↤ Submit yourselves therefore to God. Resist the devil, and he will flee from you.

James 4:7

4. The enticement to immoral conduct is sometimes subtle.

↤ For the lips of an adulteress drip honey, and smoother than oil is her speech; but in the end she is bitter as wormwood, sharp as a two-edged sword.

Proverbs 5:3–4 NASB

↤ These commands and this teaching will keep you from the immoral woman, from the smooth tongue of an adulterous woman. Don't lust for her beauty. Don't let her coyness seduce you. For a prostitute will bring you to poverty, and sleeping with another man's wife may cost you your very life. Can a man scoop fire into his lap and not be burned? Can he walk on hot coals and not blister his feet? So it is with the man who sleeps with another man's wife. He who embraces her will not go unpunished.

Proverbs 6:24–29 NLT

131

↝ Let them hold you back from an affair with an immoral woman, from listening to the flattery of an adulterous woman.

Proverbs 7:5 NLT

5. Even the suggestion of sexual immorality or impurity should be absent in Christians.

↝ But among you there must not be even a hint of sexual immorality, or of any kind of impurity, or of greed, because these are improper for God's holy people. Nor should there be obscenity, foolish talk or coarse joking, which are out of place, but rather thanksgiving.

Ephesians 5: 3–4 NIV

6. Our thoughts are an important battleground for resisting moral impurity.

↝ But I say to you that whoever looks at a woman to lust for her has already committed adultery with her in his heart.

Matthew 5:28 NKJV

↝ I made a covenant with my eyes not to look lustfully at a girl.

Job 31:1 NIV

↝ Finally, brethren, whatever things are true, whatever things are noble, whatever things are just, whatever things are pure, whatever things are lovely, whatever things are of good report, if there is any virtue and if there is anything praiseworthy—meditate on these things.

Philippians 4:8 NKJV

7. Marriage is God's provision for sexual fulfillment and purity.

↝ Marriage is honorable among all, and the bed undefiled; but fornicators and adulterers God will judge.

Hebrews 13:4 NKJV

132

✦ Drink water from your own well—share your love only with your wife. Why spill the water of your springs in public, having sex with just anyone? You should reserve it for yourselves. Don't share it with strangers. Let your wife be a fountain of blessing for you. Rejoice in the wife of your youth. She is a loving doe, a graceful deer. Let her breasts satisfy you always. May you always be captivated by her love. Why be captivated, my son, with an immoral woman, or embrace the breasts of an adulterous woman?

Proverbs 5:15–20 NLT

8. A life of immorality does not escape the judgment of God.

✦ But for the cowardly and unbelieving and abominable and murderers and immoral persons and sorcerers and idolaters and all liars, their part will be in the lake that burns with fire and brimstone, which is the second death.

Revelation 21:8 NASB

✦ We should not commit sexual immorality, as some of them did—and in one day twenty-three thousand of them died.

1 Corinthians 10:8 NIV

✦ Now the works of the flesh are evident, which are: adultery, fornication, uncleanness, licentiousness . . . those who practice such things will not inherit the kingdom of God.

Galatians 5:19, 21 NKJV

✦ For this you know, that no fornicator, unclean person, nor covetous man, who is an idolater, has any inheritance in the kingdom of Christ and of God. Let no one deceive you with empty words, for because of these things the wrath of God comes upon the sons of disobedience.

Ephesians 5:5–6 NKJV

9. Although struggles with sin are common to all humans, God has made provision for us to be forgiven through Christ.

133

↝ Who can say, "I have kept my heart pure; I am clean and without sin"?

Proverbs 20:9 NIV

↝ If we walk in the Light as He Himself is in the Light, we have fellowship with one another, and the blood of Jesus His Son cleanses us from all sin. If we say that we have no sin, we are deceiving ourselves and the truth is not in us. If we confess our sins, He is faithful and righteous to forgive us our sins and to cleanse us from all unrighteousness.

1 John 1:7–9 NASB

↝ Create in me a pure heart, O God, and renew a steadfast spirit within me.

Psalm 51:10 NIV

↝ Therefore I urge you, brethren, by the mercies of God, to present your bodies a living and holy sacrifice, acceptable to God, which is your spiritual service of worship. And do not be conformed to this world, but be transformed by the renewing of your mind, so that you may prove what the will of God is, that which is good and acceptable and perfect.

Romans 12:1–2 NASB

Prayer

Dear God, I desire that your Word be the moral compass of my life. Deliver me from spiritual complacency amid the moral disintegration that surrounds me. I desperately need your resources to live in this world in which evil is celebrated and biblical standards are mocked. Thank you that you see in me something of infinite value despite my moral shortcomings. Remake me from within that your purity might be manifest in my life. May your Holy Spirit have his way in my heart and prepare me today for tomorrow's temptations.

Promise

Submit yourselves therefore to God. Resist the devil, and he will flee from you.

James 4:7

NATURAL DISASTERS

When all things are excited to fury, and reveal their utmost power to disturb, faith smiles serenely. She is not afraid of noise, nor even of real force, she knows that the Lord stilleth the raging of the sea, and holdeth the waves in the hollow of his hand. . . . Alps and Andes may tremble, but faith rests on a firmer basis, and is not to be moved by swelling seas.

—C. H. Spurgeon, *Treasury of David, Psalm 46*

1. Natural disasters are a consequence of the entry of sin into our world and can be expected to continue until the return of Christ.

For all creation is waiting eagerly for that future day when God will reveal who his children really are. Against its will, everything on earth was subjected to God's curse. All creation anticipates the day when it will join God's children in glorious freedom from death and decay. For we know that all creation has been groaning as in the pains of childbirth right up to the present time.

Romans 8:19–22 NLT

136

2. Even though natural disasters, including floods, continue to occur in a fallen world, God's promise to Noah that he will never again destroy the whole earth with a flood still stands.

↟ The LORD smelled the soothing aroma; and the LORD said to Himself, "I will never again curse the ground on account of man, for the intent of man's heart is evil from his youth; and I will never again destroy every living thing, as I have done. While the earth remains, seedtime and harvest, and cold and heat, and summer and winter, and day and night shall not cease."

Genesis 8:21–22 NASB

↟ I establish My covenant with you; and all flesh shall never again be cut off by the water of the flood, neither shall there again be a flood to destroy the earth.

Genesis 9:11 NASB

3. Victims of natural disaster should not automatically assume that their suffering is a direct punishment for a specific sin.

↟ Or those eighteen who died when the tower in Siloam fell on them—do you think they were more guilty than all the others living in Jerusalem? I tell you, no! But unless you repent, you too will all perish.

Luke 13:4–5 NIV

4. During his earthly ministry Jesus demonstrated his unique power to control the forces of nature.

↟ And there arose a great storm of wind, and the waves beat into the ship, so that it was now full. And he was in the hinder part of the ship, asleep on a pillow: and they awake him, and say unto him, Master, carest thou not that we perish? And he arose, and rebuked the wind, and said unto the sea, Peace, be still. And the wind ceased, and there was a great calm. And he said unto them,

Why are ye so fearful? how is it that ye have no faith? And they feared exceedingly, and said one to another, What manner of man is this, that even the wind and the sea obey him?

Mark 4:37–41

↝ This is what the LORD Almighty says: "In a little while I will once more shake the heavens and the earth, the sea and the dry land."

Haggai 2:6b NIV

5. When the foundations of our lives are shaken by natural disasters, our loving God promises to be our refuge.

↝ God is our refuge and strength, a very present help in trouble. Therefore will not we fear, though the earth be removed, and though the mountains be carried into the midst of the sea; though the waters thereof roar and be troubled, though the mountains shake with the swelling thereof. . . . The LORD of hosts is with us; the God of Jacob is our refuge.

Psalm 46:1–3, 7

↝ He spoke and raised up a stormy wind, which lifted up the waves of the sea. They rose up to the heavens, they went down to the depths; their soul melted away in their misery. They fell and staggered like a drunken man, and were at their wits' end. Then they cried to the LORD in their trouble, and He brought them out of their distresses.

Psalm 107:25–28 NASB

↝ But to the poor, O LORD, you are a refuge from the storm. To the needy in distress, you are a shelter from the rain and the heat.

Isaiah 25:4 NLT

↝ The LORD is good. When trouble comes, he is a strong refuge. And he knows everyone who trusts in him.

Nahum 1:7 NLT

↝ If calamity comes upon us, whether the sword of judgment, or plague or famine, we will stand in your presence before this temple that bears your Name and will cry out to you in our distress, and you will hear us and save us.

2 Chronicles 20:9 NIV

6. No external circumstances can ever separate us from the love of God, which is ours through Christ.

Who shall separate us from the love of Christ? shall tribulation, or distress, or persecution, or famine, or nakedness, or peril, or sword? . . . For I am persuaded, that neither death, nor life, nor angels, nor principalities, nor powers, nor things present, nor things to come, nor height, nor depth, nor any other creature, shall be able to separate us from the love of God, which is in Christ Jesus our Lord.

Romans 8:35, 38–39

7. God's gifts of comfort and joy transcend external circumstances, enabling us to truly rest in the Lord, who alone is our salvation.

Even though the fig trees have no blossoms, and there are no grapes on the vine; even though the olive crop fails, and the fields lie empty and barren; even though the flocks die in the fields, and the cattle barns are empty, yet I will rejoice in the LORD! I will be joyful in the God of my salvation.

Habakkuk 3:17–18 NLT

Prayer

Father, my world is broken. I am numbed at the loss of loved ones and material things that are gone forever, and I struggle to reconcile the fact that you are a God of love with what I see around me. My inability to minister to friends and neighbors whose loss is as great or greater than mine only adds to my

139

pain. I know your Word promises that nothing can ever separate us from your love, but right now your love seems distant.

By your grace I pray that you would enable me to experience your love and comfort in the midst of the tragedy that surrounds me. Teach me that my security is in you. Enable me to take the first baby steps of faith as I place my hand in yours and trust you with my uncertain future. Energize me with your Spirit that my life may be a witness to you, my refuge.

Promise

For I am persuaded, that neither death, nor life, nor angels, nor principalities, nor powers, nor things present, nor things to come, nor height, nor depth, nor any other creature, shall be able to separate us from the love of God, which is in Christ Jesus our Lord.

Romans 8:38–39

PREPARING FOR MARRIAGE

God, knowing humankind's innate need to love and be loved, from the beginning of creation ordained a relationship in which a man and a woman could learn to meet those divinely imparted deepest needs in each other, and in so doing could discover depths of delight that could come only from the hand of a gracious God. Today you are embarking on an experience of mutual discovery and fulfillment that God longs for you to enjoy and plans for you to experience. This is a thing of wonder.

—D. Stuart Briscoe, *Baker's Wedding Handbook*

1. God designed marriage to be a permanent covenantal relationship in which a husband and wife vow to be faithful to each other for life.

The adulteress: That leaves the companion of her youth and forgets the covenant of her God.

Proverbs 2:17 NASB

141

↝ Because the LORD has been a witness between you and the wife of your youth, against whom you have dealt treacherously, though she is your companion and your wife by covenant.

Malachi 2:14 NASB

↝ Therefore what God has joined together, let man not separate.

Matthew 19:6 NIV

2. It is God's will that Christians enter into marriage covenants with fellow believers only.

↝ Nor shall you make marriages with them. You shall not give your daughter to their son, nor take their daughter for your son. For they will turn your sons away from following Me, to serve other gods.

Deuteronomy 7:3–4 NKJV (see also Exod. 34:16)

↝ Should we then hear of your doing all this great evil, transgressing against our God by marrying pagan women?

Nehemiah 13:23–27 NKJV

↝ In Judah, in Israel, and in Jerusalem there is treachery, for the men of Judah have defiled the LORD's beloved sanctuary by marrying women who worship idols. May the LORD cut off from the nation of Israel every last man who has done this and yet brings an offering to the LORD Almighty.

Malachi 2:11–12 NLT

↝ A woman is bound to her husband as long as he lives. But if her husband dies, she is free to marry anyone she wishes, but he must belong to the Lord.

1 Corinthians 7:39 NIV

↝ Don't team up with those who are unbelievers. How can goodness be a partner with wickedness? How can light live with darkness? What harmony can there be between Christ and the Devil? How can a believer be a partner with an unbeliever?

2 Corinthians 6:14–15 NLT

3. God has designed that children leave the temporary relationship of living with their parents in order to live with their marriage partner for life.

➤ For this reason a man shall leave his father and his mother, and be joined to his wife; and they shall become one flesh.

Genesis 2:24 NASB (see also Matt. 19:5; Mark 10:7–8; Eph. 5:31)

4. Marriage does not give license to abandon concern or to neglect the cultivation of a caring relationship with one's parents for life.

➤ Honor your father and your mother, that your days may be long upon the land which the LORD your God is giving you.

Exodus 20:12 NKJV

➤ Their first responsibility is to show godliness at home and repay their parents by taking care of them [widows]. This is something that pleases God very much. . . . But those who won't care for their own relatives, especially those living in the same household, have denied what we believe. Such people are worse than unbelievers.

1 Timothy 5:4, 8 NLT

5. God has designed marriage as a means to fulfill the innate human need for intimate companionship.

➤ The LORD God said, "It is not good for the man to be alone. I will make a helper suitable for him."

Genesis 2:18 NIV

➤ She is your companion and your wife by covenant.

Malachi 2:14 NKJV

6. God has designed marriage as the ordained means for sexual fulfillment.

143

↝ For this reason a man shall leave his father and his mother, and be joined to his wife; and they shall become one flesh.

Genesis 2:24 NASB

↝ Let your wife be a fountain of blessing for you. Rejoice in the wife of your youth. She is a loving doe, a graceful deer. Let her breasts satisfy you always. May you always be captivated by her love.

Proverbs 5:18–19 NLT

↝ The husband should fulfill his marital duty to his wife, and likewise the wife to her husband. The wife's body does not belong to her alone but also to her husband. In the same way, the husband's body does not belong to him alone but also to his wife.

1 Corinthians 7:3–4 NIV

↝ Marriage is to be held in honor among all, and the marriage bed is to be undefiled.

Hebrews 13:4 NASB

7. God has designed marriage as the means to propagate the human race through the birth of children.

↝ Children are a gift from the LORD; they are a reward from him.

Psalm 127:3 NLT

↝ God created man in His own image, in the image of God He created him; male and female He created them. God blessed them; and God said to them, "Be fruitful and multiply, and fill the earth, and subdue it."

Genesis 1:27–28 NASB

8. God expects wives to respectfully accept their husband's loving leadership.

↝ Submitting to one another in the fear of God. Wives, submit to your own husbands, as to the Lord. For the husband is head

144

of the wife, as also Christ is head of the church; and He is the Savior of the body. Therefore, just as the church is subject to Christ, so let the wives be to their own husbands in everything. . . . Let each one of you in particular so love his own wife as himself, and let the wife see that she respects her husband.

Ephesians 5:21–24, 33 NKJV

And the LORD God said, "It is not good for the man to be alone. I will make a companion who will help him."

Genesis 2:18 NLT

9. God requires husbands to be sacrificial and loving leaders in their homes.

Husbands, love your wives, just as Christ also loved the church and gave Himself for it, that He might sanctify and cleanse it with the washing of water by the word, that He might present it to Himself a glorious church, not having spot or wrinkle or any such thing, but that it should be holy and without blemish. So husbands ought to love their own wives as their own bodies; he who loves his wife loves himself.

Ephesians 5:25–28 NKJV

Husbands, love your wives and do not be bitter toward them.

Colossians 3:19 NKJV

10. God has provided a standard for the kind of self-giving love that should characterize marriage relationships.

Love is patient and kind. Love is not jealous or boastful or proud or rude. Love does not demand its own way. Love is not irritable, and it keeps no record of when it has been wronged. It is never glad about injustice but rejoices whenever the truth wins out. Love never gives up, never loses faith, is always hopeful, and endures through every circumstance.

1 Corinthians 13:4–7 NLT

145

11. Marriage should be approached with a conscious commitment to draw upon the supernatural resources that Christ has given for maintaining interpersonal relationships in an imperfect, fallen world.

↜ Therefore each of you must put off falsehood and speak truthfully to his neighbor, for we are all members of one body. "In your anger do not sin." Do not let the sun go down while you are still angry, and do not give the devil a foothold. . . . Do not let any unwholesome talk come out of your mouths, but only what is helpful for building others up according to their needs, that it may benefit those who listen. And do not grieve the Holy Spirit of God, with whom you were sealed for the day of redemption. Get rid of all bitterness, rage and anger, brawling and slander, along with every form of malice. Be kind and compassionate to one another, forgiving each other, just as in Christ God forgave you.

Ephesians 4:25–27, 29–32 NIV

↜ Do not merely look out for your own personal interests, but also for the interests of others.

Philippians 2:4 NASB

↜ So, as those who have been chosen of God, holy and beloved, put on a heart of compassion, kindness, humility, gentleness and patience; bearing with one another, and forgiving each other, whoever has a complaint against anyone; just as the Lord forgave you, so also should you. Beyond all these things put on love, which is the perfect bond of unity. Let the peace of Christ rule in your hearts, to which indeed you were called in one body; and be thankful.

Colossians 3:12–15 NASB

Prayer

As we anticipate with joy the vows that we will make in your presence and before family and friends, we are reminded that marriage was your idea. It was you who said it was not good for man or woman to be alone. The world seems to be telling us that monogamous marriage is an outmoded, oppressive Victorian institution. Your Word, on the contrary, affirms that marriage is a sacred and permanent union, symbolizing the mystical union between Christ and his church.

Give us a sacrificial love, Lord. Remind us that in the giving of self lies life's greatest gains. When the tuxedos are returned and the bridal gown has been preserved for posterity, we will need your grace to remain faithful to the covenant we will make on our wedding day. May our marriage and our lifelong union be a celebration of our love and the love that Christ has for his bride, the church.

Promise

The LORD God said, "It is not good for the man to be alone. I will make a helper suitable for him."

Genesis 2:18 NIV

PREPARING FOR SUNDAY WORSHIP

Acceptable worship does not happen spontaneously. Preparation is essential. In a worship service, for example, the choir prepares, the preacher prepares, and the organist and other musicians prepare. But the most important preparation of all is the preparation of the individual worshiper, and that is usually the most neglected.

—John MacArthur Jr., *The Ultimate Priority*

1. Scripture instructs us to assemble regularly for corporate worship on the first day of the week, especially as the time of Christ's return approaches.

↜ Let us consider how to stimulate one another to love and good deeds, not forsaking our own assembling together, as is the habit of some, but encouraging one another; and all the more as you see the day drawing near.

Hebrews 10:24–25 NASB

↝ They joined with the other believers and devoted themselves to the apostles' teaching and fellowship, sharing in the Lord's Supper and in prayer.

Acts 2:42 NLT

↝ On the first day of the week let each one of you lay something aside.

1 Corinthians 16:2 NKJV

2. We should not approach God in worship until we have confessed our sins.

↝ Let us draw near with a sincere heart in full assurance of faith, having our hearts sprinkled clean from an evil conscience and our bodies washed with pure water.

Hebrews 10:22 NASB

↝ Who may climb the mountain of the LORD? Who may stand in his holy place? Only those whose hands and hearts are pure, who do not worship idols and never tell lies. They will receive the LORD's blessing and have right standing with God their savior. They alone may enter God's presence and worship the God of Israel.

Psalm 24:3–6 NLT

3. Interpersonal conflicts should be resolved in order that our ability to worship be unimpeded.

↝ Therefore if thou bring thy gift to the altar, and there rememberest that thy brother hath ought against thee; leave there thy gift before the altar, and go thy way; first be reconciled to thy brother, and then come and offer thy gift.

Matthew 5:23–24

4. Our holy God should be approached in worship with a proper sense of reverence.

149

⁊⁊ Therefore, since we are receiving a kingdom that cannot be shaken, let us be thankful, and so worship God acceptably with reverence and awe, for our "God is a consuming fire."

Hebrews 12:28–29 NIV

5. Because all believers are priests, God expects us to be active participants in services of worship.

⁊⁊ [He] has made us kings and priests to His God and Father.

Revelation 1:6 NKJV

⁊⁊ You also, as living stones, are being built up a spiritual house, a holy priesthood, to offer up spiritual sacrifices acceptable to God through Jesus Christ.

1 Peter 2:5 NKJV

6. Christian worship that honors God is to be offered in spirit and in truth. Meaningless ritual displeases the Father.

⁊⁊ But the time is coming and is already here when true worshipers will worship the Father in spirit and in truth. The Father is looking for anyone who will worship him that way. For God is Spirit, so those who worship him must worship in spirit and in truth.

John 4:23–24 NLT

7. Worship on earth anticipates heavenly worship, which will occupy believers for eternity.

⁊⁊ You have come to Mount Zion, to the city of the living God, the heavenly Jerusalem, and to thousands of angels in joyful assembly.

Hebrews 12:22 NLT

⁊⁊ And when he had taken it, the four living creatures and the twenty-four elders fell down before the Lamb. Each one had a harp and they were holding golden bowls full of incense, which are the prayers of the Saints. And they sang a new song: "You are worthy to take the scroll and to open its seals, because you were slain, and with your blood you purchased men for God from every tribe and language and nation."

Revelation 5:8–9 NIV (see also vv. 10–14)

Prayer

Father, my soul longs to enter more fully into the awesome and majestic reality of worship. To die to self and be lost in worshiping you is easier said than done. I confess that I have not been preoccupied with you as I ought and my preparation for Sunday worship has been negligible. I well know that my highest duty and privilege in this life and the next is to worship my Creator. Grant me a worshiping heart, O God, that I might encounter you in all your glory. This I pray in the name of the one who alone is worthy of my worship.

Promise

Who may climb the mountain of the LORD? Who may stand in his holy place? Only those whose hands and hearts are pure, who do not worship idols and never tell lies. They will receive the LORD's blessing and have right standing with God their savior. They alone may enter God's presence and worship the God of Israel.

Psalm 24:3–6 NLT

151

REBELLIOUS CHILDREN

Our Lord is the God of the second chance. He can and will take our sons and daughters wherever they are, whatever their sins, however poorly they have lived their lives, and give them a fresh start. Often God will help them salvage their past by building on and using those very experiences that have caused hurting parents so much pain.

—Margie M. Lewis, *The Hurting Parent*

1. **Problems with children are not simply due to negative, modern cultural influences but are a consequence of the entrance of sin into the human heart. The first parents, Adam and Eve, were acquainted with this sorrow firsthand.**

⌐ Now Cain talked with Abel his brother; and it came to pass, when they were in the field, that Cain rose up against Abel his brother and killed him. Then the LORD said to Cain, "Where is Abel your brother?" And he said, "I do not know. Am I my brother's keeper?" And He said, "What have you done? The voice of your brother's blood cries out to Me from the ground. So now you are cursed from the earth, which has opened its mouth to receive your brother's blood from your hand. When you till the ground, it shall no longer yield its strength to you. A fugitive and a vagabond you shall be on the earth." And Cain said to the LORD, "My punishment is greater than I can bear!"

Genesis 4:8–13 NKJV

2. Scripture realistically records the struggles of parents in raising their children in a fallen world.

↝ Eli with Hophni and Phinehas

1 Samuel 2:12–17, 22–25; 4:11

↝ David with Absalom

2 Samuel 13–15; 18:33

↝ Manoah and his wife with Samson

Judges 13:24–14:3; 16:21–31

3. Parents are responsible before the Lord to discipline their children in love.

↝ For whom the LORD loves He reproves, even as a father corrects the son in whom he delights.

Proverbs 3:12 NASB

↝ Discipline your son while there is hope, and do not desire his death.

Proverbs 19:18 NASB

↝ Foolishness is bound up in the heart of a child; the rod of discipline will remove it far from him.

Proverbs 22:15 NASB

↝ The rod and reproof give wisdom, but a child who gets his own way brings shame to his mother.

Proverbs 29:15 NASB

153

 Fathers, don't aggravate your children. If you do, they will become discouraged and quit trying.

Colossians 3:21 NLT

 No discipline is enjoyable while it is happening—it is painful! But afterward there will be a quiet harvest of right living for those who are trained in this way.

Hebrews 12:11 NLT

4. Children who reject the godly instruction of their parents are individually responsible before the Lord. Such rejection is not simply a rebellion against parents but is at root a rebellion against God.

 Listen, my son, to your father's instruction and do not forsake your mother's teaching. They will be a garland to grace your head and a chain to adorn your neck. My son, if sinners entice you, do not give in to them.

Proverbs 1:8–10 NIV

 A wise son brings joy to his father, but a foolish son grief to his mother.

Proverbs 10:1 NIV

 A wise son heeds his father's instruction, but a mocker does not listen to rebuke.

Proverbs 13:1 NIV

 A fool spurns his father's discipline, but whoever heeds correction shows prudence.

Proverbs 15:5 NIV

5. Children who have been faithfully trained but have rejected the faith of their parents often return to that faith in later years.

↪ Train up a child in the way he should go, and when he is old he will not depart from it.

Proverbs 22:6 NKJV

↪ Being confident of this very thing, that He who has begun a good work in you will complete it until the day of Jesus Christ.

Philippians 1:6 NKJV

6. A societal characteristic of the last days is an increasing disobedience toward parents.

↪ In the last days there will be very difficult times. For people will love only themselves and their money. They will be boastful and proud, scoffing at God, disobedient to their parents, and ungrateful.

2 Timothy 3:1–2 NLT

7. The story of the prodigal son's homecoming illustrates the need for parents to continue to love their rebellious children and to be ready to receive them back with open arms.

↪ But while he was still a long way off, his father saw him and was filled with compassion for him; he ran to his son, threw his arms around him and kissed him.

Luke 15:20 NIV

↪ Love is patient, love is kind. It does not envy, it does not boast, it is not proud. It is not rude, it is not self-seeking, it is not easily angered, it keeps no record of wrongs. Love does not delight in evil but rejoices with the truth. It always protects, always trusts, always hopes, always perseveres.

1 Corinthians 13:4–7 NIV

↪ Love will cover a multitude of sins.

1 Peter 4:8 NKJV

155

8. When we are at a loss to understand the reasons why events happen in our lives, we must trust God for those things that have not been revealed to us.

↝ The secret things belong to the LORD our God, but those things which are revealed belong to us and to our children forever, that we may do all the words of this law.

Deuteronomy 29:29 NKJV

9. When our spirits are crushed with grief over a rebellious child, God's perfect peace sustains us and enables us to prayerfully await his work in the lives of our prodigals.

↝ The LORD is near to the brokenhearted and saves those who are crushed in spirit.

Psalm 34:18 NASB

↝ Rest in the LORD and wait patiently for Him.

Psalm 37:7 NASB

↝ You will keep in perfect peace all who trust in you, whose thoughts are fixed on you! Trust in the LORD always, for the LORD GOD is the eternal Rock.

Isaiah 26:3–4 NLT

↝ Don't worry about anything; instead, pray about everything. Tell God what you need, and thank him for all he has done. If you do this, you will experience God's peace, which is far more wonderful than the human mind can understand. His peace will guard your hearts and minds as you live in Christ Jesus.

Philippians 4:6–7 NLT

Prayer

God of hope, you are my only hope. We've been down this road before, Lord, but once again a heavy cloud of despair has overwhelmed me. The child you gave me has brought more pain into my life than I ever could have imagined.

God of the impossible, please salvage the past and make something of the wreckage that remains of my child's life. I am grateful that your ability to work in the life of my child does not depend on my resources, because mine are spent. Right now I release my child to you. I entrust the future of my prodigal into the hand of the one who loves my child even more than I do. Enable me to forgive, accept, and love my child—and to hope again.

Promise

The LORD is near to the brokenhearted and saves those who are crushed in spirit.

Psalm 34:18 NASB

RESISTING TEMPTATION

Often we feel today like our reservoir of strength is not going to last for another day. The fact is, it won't. Today's resources are for today, and part of those resources is the confidence that new resources will be given tomorrow.

—John Piper, *A Godward Life*

1. Temptation is a reality that began in the Garden of Eden. Adam and Eve were tempted by Satan to disobey God's command not to eat of the forbidden fruit.

> When the woman saw that the fruit of the tree was good for food and pleasing to the eye, and also desirable for gaining wisdom, she took some and ate it. She also gave some to her husband, who was with her, and he ate it.
>
> Genesis 3:6 NIV (see also vv. 1–5, 7)

2. Giving in to temptation can have grave consequences, as illustrated in the sin of Adam and Eve. It affected their relationships with God, with each other, and with the environment around them.

> ✴ When the man and his wife heard the sound of the LORD God as he was walking in the garden in the cool of the day, and they hid from the LORD God among the trees of the garden. . . . "Cursed is the ground because of you; through painful toil you will eat of it all the days of your life. It will produce thorns and thistles for you, and you will eat the plants of the field. By the sweat of your brow you will eat your food until you return to the ground, since from it you were taken."
>
> Genesis 3:8, 17–19 NIV (see also vv. 9–16)

3. Resisting strong temptation may necessitate removing ourselves from the scene of the temptation.

> ✴ She kept putting pressure on him day after day, but he refused to sleep with her, and he kept out of her way as much as possible. One day, however, no one else was around when he was doing his work inside the house. She came and grabbed him by his shirt, demanding, "Sleep with me!" Joseph tore himself away, but as he did, his shirt came off. She was left holding it as he ran from the house.
>
> Genesis 39:10–12 NLT

> ✴ Run from her! Don't go near the door of her house!
>
> Proverbs 5:8 NLT

> ✴ Be of sober spirit, be on the alert. Your adversary, the devil, prowls around like a roaring lion, seeking someone to devour. But resist him, firm in your faith, knowing that the same experiences of suffering are being accomplished by your brethren who are in the world.
>
> 1 Peter 5:8–9 NASB

> ✴ Put away perversity from your mouth; keep corrupt talk far from your lips. Let your eyes look straight ahead, fix your gaze directly before you. Make level paths for your feet and take only

Resisting Temptation

ways that are firm. Do not swerve to the right or the left; keep
your feet from evil.

Proverbs 4:24–27 NIV

4. Jesus drew upon Scripture to resist temptation from Satan.

⁓ The Scriptures say . . . the Scriptures say . . . the Scriptures
say . . .

Matthew 4:1–11 NLT

⁓ Because he himself suffered when he was tempted, he is able
to help those who are being tempted.

Hebrews 2:18 NIV

⁓ This High Priest of ours understands our weaknesses, for he
faced all of the same temptations we do, yet he did not sin. So
let us come boldly to the throne of our gracious God. There we
will receive his mercy, and we will find grace to help us when we
need it.

Hebrews 4:15–16 NLT

⁓ Lead us not into temptation.

Matthew 6:13

5. The source of temptation is not God but rather our sinful desires.

⁓ Let no one say when he is tempted, "I am being tempted by
God"; for God cannot be tempted by evil, and He Himself does
not tempt anyone. But each one is tempted when he is carried
away and enticed by his own lust. Then when lust has conceived, it gives birth to sin; and when sin is accomplished, it
brings forth death.

James 1:13–15 NASB

⁓ People who long to be rich fall into temptation and are trapped
by many foolish and harmful desires that plunge them into ruin
and destruction. But the love of money is at the root of all kinds

160

of evil. And some people, craving money, have wandered from the faith and pierced themselves with many sorrows.

1 Timothy 6:9–10 NLT

↝ They believe for a while, and in time of temptation fall away.

Luke 8:13 NASB

↝ I was afraid that in some way the tempter might have tempted you and our efforts might have been useless.

1 Thessalonians 3:5 NIV

6. Our faithful God never allows us to be tempted beyond our ability to resist in his strength.

↝ Remember that the temptations that come into your life are no different from what others experience. And God is faithful. He will keep the temptation from becoming so strong that you can't stand up against it. When you are tempted, he will show you a way out so that you will not give in to it.

1 Corinthians 10:13 NLT

↝ The Lord knows how to rescue the godly from temptation.

2 Peter 2:9 NASB

↝ Pray that you will not fall into temptation.

Luke 22:40 NIV

7. On those occasions when we succumb to temptation and fall into sin, we should be quick to confess our sins and, with a repentant heart, receive the Lord's forgiveness.

↝ If we confess our sins, He is faithful and just to forgive us our sins and to cleanse us from all unrighteousness.

1 John 1:9 NKJV

161

↤ I acknowledged my sin to You, and my iniquity I have not hidden. I said, "I will confess my transgressions to the LORD," and You forgave the iniquity of my sin.

Psalm 32:5 NKJV

Prayer

I bow before you, Lord, asking for your strength to meet the temptations that face me today and will face me tomorrow. I desire to please you and resist temptation, but as you well know, I have failed miserably. Forgive me for the times I have been weak because I have not availed myself of your resources. Thank you for the example of Christ, who resisted Satan's temptation with your Word. Enable me to so saturate my mind with Scripture that it will likewise become for me a useful weapon in resisting Satan's attacks. Thank you for the promise that you will not allow me to be tempted beyond my ability to resist. The next time I'm tempted, help me to find your way out. I ask this in the name of the one who resisted the temptation to come down from the cross.

Promise

Remember that the temptations that come into your life are no different from what others experience. And God is faithful. He will keep the temptation from becoming so strong that you can't stand up against it. When you are tempted, he will show you a way out so that you will not give in to it.

1 Corinthians 10:13 NLT

USING SCRIPTURE IN DAILY LIFE

A sentence, a phrase, even a single word of Scripture, applied by the Spirit of God, can sustain us for hours, days, and weeks in time of need. . . . As myriad drops of dew reflect the sun's rays, each with a similar yet totally differing glory, so tiny bits and pieces of Scripture reflect new facets of radiance from long-loved truths to illumine new phases of old sorrows and meet our recurring needs.

—Margaret Clarkson, *Grace Grows Best in Winter*

1. Scripture can always be trusted because it is the inspired, truthful, and timeless Word of God.

And we will never stop thanking God that when we preached his message to you, you didn't think of the words we spoke as being just our own. You accepted what we said as the very word of God—which, of course, it was. And this word continues to work in you who believe.

1 Thessalonians 2:13 NLT

163

🙰 The Scripture cannot be broken.

John 10:35

🙰 All Scripture is given by inspiration of God.

2 Timothy 3:16 NKJV

🙰 But know this first of all, that no prophecy of Scripture is a matter of one's own interpretation, for no prophecy was ever made by an act of human will, but men moved by the Holy Spirit spoke from God.

2 Peter 1:20–21 NASB

2. To understand what God desires to communicate to us, we must give careful attention to Scripture.

🙰 He read it aloud from daybreak till noon as he faced the square before the Water Gate in the presence of the men, women and others who could understand. And all the people listened attentively to the Book of the Law. . . . They read from the Book of the Law of God, making it clear and giving the meaning so that the people could understand what was being read.

Nehemiah 8:3, 8 NIV

3. When the seed of Scripture is planted in receptive hearts, it takes root and produces fruit.

🙰 Now the parable is this: The seed is the word of God. Those by the wayside are the ones who hear; then the devil comes and takes away the word out of their hearts, lest they should believe and be saved. But the ones on the rock are those who, when they hear, receive the word with joy; and these have no root, who believe for a while and in time of temptation fall away. And the ones that fell among thorns are those who, when they have heard, go out and are choked with cares, riches, and pleasures of life, and bring no fruit to maturity. But the ones that fell on the good ground are those who, having heard the word with a noble and good heart, keep it and bear fruit with patience.

Luke 8:11–15 NKJV

4. The children who are raised in our homes should be trained in the Scripture from their earliest years.

↞ And you must commit yourselves wholeheartedly to these commands I am giving you today. Repeat them again and again to your children. Talk about them when you are at home and when you are away on a journey, when you are lying down and when you are getting up again. Tie them to your hands as a reminder, and wear them on your forehead. Write them on the doorposts of your house and on your gates.

Deuteronomy 6:6–9 NLT

↞ From infancy you have known the holy Scriptures, which are able to make you wise for salvation through faith in Christ Jesus.

2 Timothy 3:15 NIV

5. Scripture is intended to be useful for teaching, reproof, correction, and training.

↞ All Scripture is inspired by God and profitable for teaching, for reproof, for correction, for training in righteousness; so that the man of God may be adequate, equipped for every good work.

2 Timothy 3:16–17 NASB

↞ Let the word of Christ dwell in you richly as you teach and admonish one another with all wisdom, and as you sing psalms, hymns and spiritual songs with gratitude in your hearts to God.

Colossians 3:16 NIV

6. Scripture should be the object of our meditation, both in the day and in the night hours.

↞ I rise before the dawning of the morning, and cry for help; I hope in Your word. My eyes are awake through the night watches, that I may meditate on Your word.

Psalm 119:147–148 NKJV

➳ This Book of the Law shall not depart from your mouth, but you shall meditate in it day and night, that you may observe to do according to all that is written in it. For then you will make your way prosperous, and then you will have good success.

Joshua 1:8 NKJV

7. Scripture functions as a guide to illumine our path.

➳ The commands of the LORD are clear, giving insight to life.

Psalm 19:8b NLT

➳ Direct my footsteps according to your word; let no sin rule over me.

Psalm 119:133 NIV

➳ For the commandment is a lamp; and the law is light; and reproofs of instruction are the way of life.

Proverbs 6:23

8. Our constant intake of Scripture helps to preserve our moral purity when facing temptation.

➳ Moreover by them is thy servant warned: and in keeping of them there is great reward.

Psalm 19:11

➳ How can a young man keep his way pure? By keeping it according to Your word. . . . Your word I have treasured in my heart, that I may not sin against You. . . . Establish my footsteps in Your Word, and do not let any iniquity have dominion over me.

Psalm 119: 9, 11, 133 NASB

➳ For the word of God is full of living power. It is sharper than the sharpest knife, cutting deep into our innermost thoughts and desires. It exposes us for what we really are.

Hebrews 4:12 NLT

9. Scripture is given to us with the expectation that we obey its instructions.

⁓ But the word is very near you, in your mouth and in your heart, that you may do it.

Deuteronomy 30:14 NKJV

⁓ By them is your servant warned; in keeping them there is great reward.

Psalm 19:11 NIV

⁓ Happy are people of integrity, who follow the law of the LORD. Happy are those who obey his decrees and search for him with all their hearts.

Psalm 119:1–2 NLT

10. Scripture helps us distinguish good from evil.

⁓ For though by this time you ought to be teachers, you have need again for someone to teach you the elementary principles of the oracles of God, and you have come to need milk and not solid food. For everyone who partakes only of milk is not accustomed to the word of righteousness, for he is an infant. But solid food is for the mature, who because of practice have their senses trained to discern good and evil.

Hebrews 5:12–14 NASB

11. Scripture strengthens us in times of sorrow and weakness.

⁓ My soul weeps because of grief; strengthen me according to Your word.

Psalm 119:28 NASB

⁓ I have remembered Your ordinances from of old, O LORD, and comfort myself.

Psalm 119:52 NASB

167

⌐ If Your law had not been my delight, then I would have per-
ished in my affliction. I will never forget Your precepts, for by
them You have revived me.

Psalm 119:92–93 NASB

12. Scripture should be part of our regular diet of spir-
itual nourishment.

⌐ You must crave pure spiritual milk so that you can grow into
the fullness of your salvation. Cry out for this nourishment as
a baby cries for milk, now that you have had a taste of the
Lord's kindness.

1 Peter 2:2–3 NLT

Prayer

Lord, I need to be reminded that there is no such thing as instant
godliness. I confess that I have not been disciplined in my intake
of Scripture and my prayers for victory over sin have been hypo-
critical. Enable me now to approach your Word in a spirit of humility and contrition. With dependence upon your Holy Spirit, I
ask for the will to be disciplined in my intake and meditation
upon your life-giving Word. Thank you for the treasure that is
mine in the pages of Scripture.

Promise

So will My word be which goes forth from My mouth; it will not
return to Me empty, without accomplishing what I desire, and
without succeeding in the matter for which I sent it.

Isaiah 55:11 NASB

WISDOM FOR MAKING DECISIONS

How long is it since you read right through the Bible? Do you spend as much time with the Bible each day as you do even with the newspaper? What fools some of us are!—and we remain fools all our lives, simply because we will not take the trouble to do what has to be done to receive the wisdom which is God's free gift.

—J. I. Packer, *Knowing God*

1. Our Lord is a rich source of unlimited wisdom.

↬ He giveth wisdom unto the wise, and knowledge to them that know understanding: He revealeth the deep and secret things: he knoweth what is in the darkness, and the light dwelleth with him.

Daniel 2:21–22

↬ Your word is a lamp to my feet and a light to my path.

Psalm 119:105 NKJV

↬ Oh, the depth of the riches of the wisdom and knowledge of God! How unsearchable his judgments, and his paths beyond tracing out! Who has known the mind of the Lord? Or who has been his counselor?

Romans 11:33–34 NIV

↵ Christ, in whom are hidden all the treasures of wisdom and knowledge.

Colossians 2:3 NIV

↵ Worthy is the Lamb that was slain to receive power, and riches, and wisdom, and strength, and honour, and glory, and blessing.

Revelation 5:12

2. The wisdom that comes from the Lord is superior and set apart from earthly wisdom because it is pure, peace loving, and gentle.

↵ For jealousy and selfishness are not God's kind of wisdom. Such things are earthly, unspiritual, and motivated by the Devil.

James 3:15 NLT

↵ But the wisdom that comes from heaven is first of all pure. It is also peace loving, gentle at all times, and willing to yield to others. It is full of mercy and good deeds. It shows no partiality and is always sincere.

James 3:17 NLT

3. Wisdom that comes from God is available to those who ask in faith.

↵ If any of you lacks wisdom, let him ask of God, who gives to all liberally and without reproach, and it will be given to him. But let him ask in faith, with no doubting, for he who doubts is like a wave of the sea driven and tossed by the wind.

James 1:5–6 NKJV

↵ If you accept my words . . . , turning your ear to wisdom and applying your heart to understanding, and if you call out for insight and cry aloud for understanding, and if you look for it as for silver and search for it as for hidden treasure, then you will understand the fear of the LORD and find the knowl-

170

edge of God. For the LORD gives wisdom, and from his mouth come knowledge and understanding.

Proverbs 2:1–6 NIV

✦ Trust in the LORD with all your heart; do not depend on your own understanding. Seek his will in all you do, and he will direct your paths.

Proverbs 3:5–6 NLT

4. God is to be approached with humility and reverence if we desire his wisdom for decision making.

✦ Pride leads to disgrace, but with humility comes wisdom.

Proverbs 11:2 NLT

✦ The fear of the LORD is the beginning of wisdom; a good understanding have all those who do His commandments.

Psalm 111:10 NKJV

✦ This is what the LORD says: "Let not the wise man boast of his wisdom or the strong man boast of his strength or the rich man boast of his riches, but let him who boasts boast about this: that he understands and knows me, that I am the LORD, who exercises kindness, justice and righteousness on earth, for in these I delight," declares the LORD.

Jeremiah 9:23–24 NIV

✦ Where is the wise? Where is the scribe? Where is the disputer of this age? Has not God made foolish the wisdom of this world?

1 Corinthians 1:20 NKJV

✦ For you see your calling, brethren, that not many wise according to the flesh, not many mighty, not many noble, are called. But God has chosen the foolish things of the world to put to shame the wise, and God has chosen the weak things of the world to put to shame the things which are mighty. . . . that no flesh should glory in His presence.

1 Corinthians 1:26–27, 29 NKJV

5. One way to increase in wisdom is to cultivate friendships with wise people.

171

➤ Whoever walks with the wise will become wise; whoever walks with fools will suffer harm.

Proverbs 13:20 NLT

6. Our decisions should be based on a sincere desire to bring glory to Christ in all we do and say.

➤ And whatever you do or say, let it be as a representative of the Lord Jesus, all the while giving thanks through him to God the Father.

Colossians 3:17 NLT

➤ Therefore, whether you eat or drink, or whatever you do, do all to the glory of God.

1 Corinthians 10:31 NKJV

Prayer

Father, I come before your throne knowing that you are the ultimate source of all wisdom. In the decisions that face me now, I humbly turn to you for wisdom. I need more than fallible human reason and understanding. I acknowledge that reverence for you is the beginning of wisdom, and therefore I pray that your Spirit will control my decision-making process. May my choices glorify you. This I pray through Christ in whom are hidden all the treasures of wisdom and knowledge.

Promise

If any of you lacks wisdom, let him ask of God, who gives to all liberally and without reproach, and it will be given to him. But let him ask in faith, with no doubting, for he who doubts is like a wave of the sea driven and tossed by the wind.

James 1:5–6 NKJV

WORK AND LEISURE

There is not one reference in the entire New Testament saying (or even implying) that Jesus intensely worked and labored in an occupation to the point of emotional exhaustion. . . . There are several times when we are told He deliberately took a break. . . . His was a life of beautiful balance. He accomplished everything the Father sent Him to do. Everything. And he did it without ignoring those essential times of leisure. If that is the way He lived, then it makes good sense that is the way we, too, must learn to live.

—Charles R. Swindoll, *Leisure: Having Fun Is Serious Business*

1. God originally created work as a meaningful part of human life in a perfect world.

⁀ The LORD God took the man and put him in the Garden of Eden to work it and take care of it.

Genesis 2:15 NIV

173

2. The entrance of sin into the world led to God's curse on the ground itself. The burden of work necessary to sustain life was greatly increased.

↝ Because you listened to your wife and ate the fruit I told you not to eat, I have placed a curse on the ground. All your life you will struggle to scratch a living from it. It will grow thorns and thistles for you, though you will eat of its grains. All your life you will sweat to produce food, until your dying day. Then you will return to the ground from which you came. For you were made from dust, and to the dust you will return.

Genesis 3:17–19 NLT

3. God's intended pattern is for us to work six days a week and rest from that work one day each week.

↝ And on the seventh day God ended His work which He had done, and He rested on the seventh day from all His work which He had done. Then God blessed the seventh day and sanctified it, because in it He rested from all His work which God had created and made.

Genesis 2:2–3 NKJV

↝ Remember to observe the Sabbath day by keeping it holy. Six days a week are set apart for your daily duties and regular work, but the seventh day is a day of rest dedicated to the LORD your God. . . . For in six days the LORD made the heavens, the earth, the sea, and everything in them; then he rested on the seventh day. That is why the LORD blessed the Sabbath day and set it apart as holy.

Exodus 20:8–11 NLT

↝ Six days you are to do your work, but on the seventh day you shall cease from labor so that your ox and your donkey may rest, and the son of your female slave, as well as your stranger, may refresh themselves.

Exodus 23:12 NASB

4. Work can become meaningless when it's performed exclusively for material ends.

⟶ Man does not live by bread alone, but man lives by everything that proceeds out the mouth of the LORD.

Deuteronomy 8:3 NASB

⟶ So I turned in despair from hard work. It was not the answer to my search for satisfaction in this life. For though I do my work with wisdom, knowledge, and skill, I must leave everything I gain to people who haven't worked to earn it. This is not only foolish but highly unfair. So what do people get for all their hard work? Their days of labor are filled with pain and grief; even at night they cannot rest. It is all utterly meaningless.

Ecclesiastes 2:20–23 NLT

⟶ Why do you spend money for what is not bread, and your wages for what does not satisfy?

Isaiah 55:2 NKJV

⟶ Do not labor for the food which perishes, but for the food which endures to everlasting life, which the Son of Man will give you, because God the Father has set His seal on Him.

John 6:27 NKJV

5. Work is meaningful when it's consciously motivated by a desire to glorify God.

⟶ A man can do nothing better than to eat and drink and find satisfaction in his work. This too, I see, is from the hand of God. . . . Everyone may eat and drink, and find satisfaction in all his toil—this is the gift of God.

Ecclesiastes 2:24; 3:13 NIV

⟶ Therefore, my beloved brethren, be steadfast, immovable, always abounding in the work of the Lord, knowing that your labor is not in vain in the Lord.

1 Corinthians 15:58 NKJV

175

↝ Whatever you do in word or deed, do all in the name of the Lord Jesus, giving thanks through Him to God the Father. . . . Whatever you do, do your work heartily, as for the Lord rather than for men.

Colossians 3:17, 23 NASB

6. Scripture warns us about the dangers of laziness.

↝ Diligent hands will rule, but laziness ends in slave labor.

Proverbs 12:24 NIV

↝ Laziness brings on deep sleep, and the shiftless man goes hungry.

Proverbs 19:15 NIV

↝ Laziness lets the roof leak, and soon the rafters begin to rot.

Ecclesiastes 10:18 NLT

↝ Never be lazy in your work, but serve the Lord enthusiastically.

Romans 12:11 NLT

↝ For even when we were with you, we used to give you this order: if anyone is not willing to work, then he is not to eat, either. For we hear that some among you are leading an undisciplined life, doing no work at all, but acting like busybodies. Now such persons we command and exhort in the Lord Jesus Christ to work in quiet fashion and eat their own bread.

2 Thessalonians 3:10–12 NASB

↝ If you are a thief, stop stealing. Begin using your hands for honest work, and then give generously to others in need.

Ephesians 4:28 NLT

7. God expects us to make rest a priority in our lives.

↝ It is useless for you to work so hard from early morning until late at night, anxiously working for food to eat; for God gives rest to his loved ones.

Psalm 127:2 NLT

↵ Do not wear yourself out to get rich; have the wisdom to show restraint.

Proverbs 23:4 NIV

↵ And He said to them, "Come aside by yourselves to a deserted place and rest a while." For there were many coming and going, and they did not even have time to eat.

Mark 6:31 NKJV

↵ Now when it was day, He departed and went into a deserted place.

Luke 4:42 NKJV

↵ Come to me, all you who are weary and burdened, and I will give you rest. Take my yoke upon you and learn from me, for I am gentle and humble in heart, and you will find rest for your souls.

Matthew 11:28–29 NIV

8. Ultimately God will reward us for the work we have done with a conscious desire to please him.

↵ Work hard, but not just to please your masters when they are watching. As slaves of Christ, do the will of God with all your heart. Work with enthusiasm, as though you were working for the Lord rather than for people. Remember that the Lord will reward each one of us for the good we do, whether we are slaves or free.

Ephesians 6:6–8 NLT

↵ Whatever you do, work at it with all your heart, as working for the Lord, not for men, since you know that you will receive an inheritance from the Lord as a reward. It is the Lord Christ you are serving.

Colossians 3:23–25 NIV

↵ Therefore we also have as our ambition, whether at home or absent, to be pleasing to Him. For we must all appear before the judgment seat of Christ, so that each one may be recompensed for his deeds in the body, according to what he has done, whether good or bad.

2 Corinthians 5:9–10 NASB

↶ And let the beauty of the LORD our God be upon us, and establish the work of our hands for us; yes, establish the work of our hands.

Psalm 90:17 NKJV

Prayer

Lord, I need to guard against the overloading pressure of the world at my door. Too often I have been guilty of burning the candle at both ends and equating busyness with your will.

Certainly it was your design that work and rest complement each other. Thank you that my daily labors can be performed as acts of worship, pleasing and acceptable to you. It is my desire to pour out my devotion to you in the vocation to which you have called me. Enable me to cultivate a balanced and biblical lifestyle. Help me to discipline myself to be still before you, to enjoy the blessings of family and friends, and to make rest a priority. May your Sabbath be always a delight to my body and soul, a preparation for worship and service in this life and the next.

Promise

It is useless for you to work so hard from early morning until late at night, anxiously working for food to eat; for God gives rest to his loved ones.

Psalm 127:2 NLT

WORRY AND ANXIETY

It is not only wrong to worry; it is infidelity, because worry-ing means that we do not think that God can look after the practical details of our lives. . . . Deliberately tell God that you will not fret about that thing. All our fret and worry is caused by calculating without God. . . .

—Oswald Chambers, *My Utmost for His Highest*

1. Scripture repeatedly warns us to avoid the sin of worry.

↝ "Do not worry . . . do not worry . . . do not worry."

Matthew 6:25, 31, 34 NIV

↝ Don't worry about anything.

Philippians 4:6 NLT

2. There is a proper place for legitimate concern in the life of the believer.

↝ There should be no division in the body, but that its parts should have equal concern for each other. If one part suffers,

179

every part suffers with it; if one part is honored, every part rejoices with it.

1 Corinthians 12:25–26 NIV

↝ For I have no one else of kindred spirit who will genuinely be
concerned for your welfare.

Philippians 2:20 NASB

↝ Apart from such external things, there is the daily pressure on
me of concern for all the churches.

2 Corinthians 11:28 NASB

3. We demonstrate our faith in God's providential care of his children as we share our needs with him in prayer.

↝ Give all your worries and cares to God, for he cares about
what happens to you.

1 Peter 5:7 NLT

↝ Look at the birds of the air, for they neither sow nor reap nor
gather into barns; yet your heavenly Father feeds them. Are you
not of more value than they? . . . So why do you worry about
clothing? Consider the lilies of the field, how they grow: they neither toil nor spin; and yet I say to you that even Solomon in all
his glory was not arrayed like one of these. Now if God so clothes
the grass of the field, which today is, and tomorrow is thrown into
the oven, will He not much more clothe you, O you of little faith?

Matthew 6:26, 28–30 NKJV

4. Prayer is an appointed means by which we can share our concerns with the Lord lest they become a source of anxiety.

↝ Don't worry about anything; instead, pray about everything.
Tell God what you need, and thank him for all he has done. If
you do this, you will experience God's peace, which is far more

wonderful than the human mind can understand. His peace will guard your hearts and minds as you live in Christ Jesus.

Philippians 4:6–7 NLT

✎ Give your burdens to the LORD, and he will take care of you. He will not permit the godly to slip and fall.

Psalm 55:22 NLT

5. God calls us to commit our worries about tomorrow to him and to concentrate our energies on the work to which he calls us today.

✎ So do not worry, saying, "What shall we eat?" or "What shall we drink?" or "What shall we wear?" For the pagans run after all these things, and your heavenly Father knows that you need them. But seek first his kingdom and his righteousness, and all these things will be given to you as well. Therefore do not worry about tomorrow, for tomorrow will worry about itself. Each day has enough trouble of its own.

Matthew 6:31–34 NIV

✎ Give us this day our daily bread.

Matthew 6:11

6. God can use our words of encouragement, especially those based on Scripture, to alleviate the weight of worry in others.

✎ Worry weighs a person down; an encouraging word cheers a person up.

Proverbs 12:25 NLT

Prayer

How easily I am consumed with worry. My human tendency is to fear the worst in spite of the fact that your Word tells me to be

181

anxious for nothing. Today I need to hope in you more than ever. Snatch me, I pray, from this overpowering current of anxiety and worry and remind me that you are still my faithful God. Enable me to release my cares into your loving care. I desperately need your touch of joy in my life. Help me not to allow the worries of tomorrow to rob me of the peace that you want me to have today.

Promise

Don't worry about anything; instead, pray about everything. Tell God what you need, and thank him for all he has done. If you do this, you will experience God's peace, which is far more wonderful than the human mind can understand. His peace will guard your hearts and minds as you live in Christ Jesus.

Philippians 4:6–7 NLT

Paul E. Engle is an ordained minister who has served churches in Pennsylvania, Connecticut, Illinois, and Michigan and has also taught in several seminaries as a visiting instructor. He holds degrees from Houghton College, Wheaton College Graduate School, and Westminster Theological Seminary. He is the author of several books.

Margie W. Engle is an experienced schoolteacher, having taught in Pennsylvania, Illinois, and Michigan. She holds degrees from Geneva College and Southern Connecticut State University. She and Paul are the parents of two daughters.